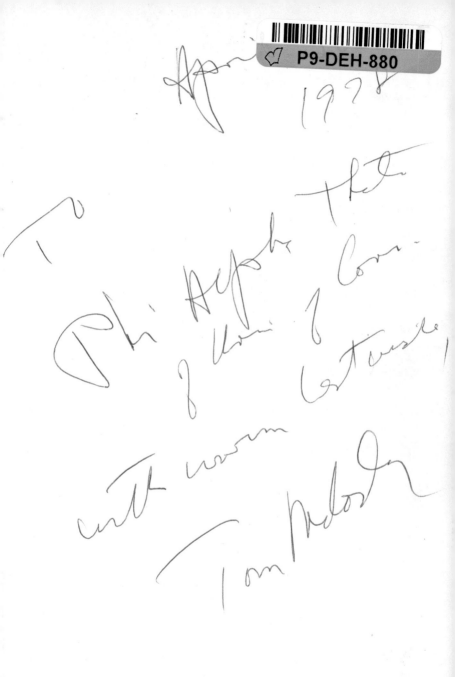

IDI AMIN DADA: HITLER IN AFRICA

Idi Amin Dada: His Excellency President for Life Field Marshal Al Hadji Dr. Idi Amin Dada, VC, DSO, MC, Lord of All the Beasts of the Earth and Fishes of the Sea and Conqueror of the British Empire in Africa in General and Uganda in Particular.

IDI AMIN DADA: HITLER IN AFRICA

Thomas and Margaret Melady

SHEED ANDREWS AND McMEEL

SUBSIDIARY OF UNIVERSAL PRESS SYNDICATE
KANSAS CITY

Library of Congress Cataloging in Publication Data

Melady, Thomas Patrick.
  Idi Amin Dada: Hitler in Africa.

  1. Amin, Idi, 1925–   2. Uganda—Presidents—
Biography. 3. Uganda—Politics and government—
1962–   4. Melady, Thomas Patrick. 5. Melady,
Margaret Badum. I. Melady, Margaret Badum, joint
author.
DT433.282.A55M44   967.6'104'0924 [B]   77-11706
ISBN 0-8362-0783-1

This book is dedicated

to

the memories of Joe, Benedicto, Clement, and Archbishop Luwum who were friends, and to the hundreds of thousands of other men and women who have been killed in Uganda during the Amin regime.

CONTENTS

1: DIPLOMATIC ASSIGNMENT: KAMPALA, UGANDA

AS THE REPRESENTATIVE OF THE PRESIDENT OF THE UNITED States, I had to deal with Idi Amin Dada, president of Uganda. I am pleased to say that I was the last U.S. ambassador to his government, and I hope that there will be no others. For tyrants do not change; they only become more brutal. The tortures, killings, and atrocities do not stop; they increase.

Brutal tyrants are known to lie. They do not hesitate to distort and totally fabricate circumstances. At the same time, they are cunning. They like to play with people, especially those they eventually plan to liquidate.

Tyrants are often obsessed with sex. Victims of their oppression are frequently forced to submit to personal degradation, abuse, and cruel sexual mutilation.

Finally, brutal tyrants select easily identifiable minority communities to bear the brunt of the pressures and hatreds of the majority.

These were the characteristics of the tyrant Adolf Hitler and other members of the Third Reich. And they are the characteristics of Idi Amin and his henchmen.

Uganda was my third diplomatic assignment. I had served as U.S. ambassador to Burundi and senior adviser to the U.S. Delegation to the 1970 United Nations General Assembly. My wife, Margaret, and I knew that Uganda would most likely be our last diplomatic post, for we were only in the foreign service temporarily. I was not a career diplomat.

After I received my Ph.D. from Catholic University in political science and economics, I began to specialize in Afro-Asian affairs. I was especially interested in contemporary Third World nationalism. Talent scouts in both the Johnson and Nixon administrations had been in contact with me about serving as an ambassador.

In 1969, when I was contacted by the White House, I was serving as professor of Afro-Asian affairs at Seton Hall University in New Jersey. Margaret and I felt that it was the right time for us to go overseas. Friends associated with then-Governor

1

Nelson Rockefeller endorsed my candidacy. (I had worked for the Rockefeller campaign when he was seeking the Republican nomination for the presidency in 1968.) In September 1969, the White House announced my appointment to Burundi. Seton Hall University authorities gave me a four-year leave. When I was to return to the Seton Hall campus in the fall of 1973, four years later, I had had the experience not only of an attempted coup d'état and its aftermath in Burundi, but of personally dealing with a confirmed dictator who directed the torture and murder of thousands of people in Uganda. Some of our personal friends were among those murdered.

We had visited Uganda briefly for the first time in July 1962, eight months after our marriage in December 1961. It was through Ugandan friends that we first met each other in the fall of 1960. Margaret, then a senior at the College of New Rochelle, had originally accepted an invitation to teach at the girls' high school in Masaka, Uganda, after graduation in 1961. Instead we were married a few months later.

Against the background of those beautiful memories we went to Uganda in 1972. Within ninety days of arriving, I was to be in the presence of a man who had said that Hitler knew how to take care of the Jews. The ugliness quickly became real. Within a few weeks, Amin directed the murder of our friend, Father Clement Kiggundu. Shortly after that, Joseph Mubiru, who had introduced Margaret and me to each other while he was the president of the African Catholic Student Organization in New York City in 1960, also was murdered. By October 1972, we prayed daily for an end to the suffering of the Ugandan people.

Was this the same Uganda—loved by so many—a country known for its culture, charm, and beauty? Once it had been a favorite place for tourists who were interested in the numerous wild game and magnificent natural settings. It had attracted visiting academicians throughout the world, for it was the center of East African higher education. Located in the center of the African continent, it was the point of convergence of north with south, and east with west. The Entebbe airport was a needed refueling point on the long trips up and down the African continent.

2

Dr. and Mrs. Melady with daughters upon arrival at Entebbe airport on July 25, 1972, being welcomed by officials of Ministry of Foreign Affairs.

Uganda was of interest to political scientists because of the challenge of understanding the workings of a society in which there existed different levels of political understanding and ability.

When we arrived in Uganda, we knew that the chief of state was an authoritarian military leader who had seized power with a military takeover. Uganda became one of the twenty African states being ruled by military governments. By the time we left in 1973 we knew that Idi Amin Dada was directing a holocaust in Uganda. The enormity of the presence of a man personally responsible for ongoing murders made us shudder.

I was called to the military command post to see Amin three days before Christmas in 1972. Amin's purpose in summoning me was to brief me on a telegram which he had sent to President Richard Nixon.

The issue was the resumption of U.S. aircraft bombings on North Vietnam. The two-page telegram criticized the U.S. position for its indiscriminate bombings and for threatening the spirit of negotiation. The document described U.S. action as ''barbarity which has no parallel in the history of mankind.'' Copies of the telegram were sent to President Nikolai Podgorny of the Soviet Union, Mao Tse-tung in China, the United Nations, and the Organization of African Unity. The telegram itself was obviously not written by Amin. Its wording and phraseology were not the usual bombastic language of Amin. Its ideas and points were entirely those of North Vietnam and its allies. It would not be surprising if the Soviets, another Eastern bloc embassy, or a Uganda government official sympathetic to the Communist cause had suggested the issue to Amin.

Amin sent another telegram to President Nixon in early February. This time he hailed the Vietnamese for fighting ''U.S. aggressors and the puppet regime who are in the pockets of the imperialist. . . . You should now leave the Vietnamese people alone. . . . You should leave off Vietnam and leave the Vietnamese people to solve their own problems. The Vietnamese people are no longer sleeping and they are not alone in the fight against imperialism.'' The telegram, however, was never received directly by the White House. The message was reported in

Kampala and relayed by the embassy. The wording of this telegram was definitely Amin's.

On the morning of February 8, 1973, I received a message from the State Department to return to Washington immediately for consultations. The U.S. had also withdrawn its ambassadors from Sweden and India as a sign of its displeasure over the comments of those governments about our Vietnamese position. When the ambassadors departed from those countries, the U.S. government made a clear announcement of the reason.

But in the case of Uganda, I was quietly withdrawn for consultations. No announcement was made at the time. When I returned to Washington, I learned that there were those in our government who were more concerned about Amin's statements on Vietnam than his brutal tyrannical regime. I argued that our embassy should eventually be closed and our ambassador be withdrawn, not for Amin's statements on Vietnam, but rather to show our disapproval of his ongoing genocide against his own people and the disregard for the lives of those foreigners living in Uganda. I, therefore, believed that the embassy should remain long enough to calmly withdraw as many people as possible. I suggested that the task be completed by September 1973. I succeeded only partially in having my plan accepted. The embassy did indeed prepare to withdraw its AID personnel and attempted to convince as many missionaries as possible to leave. However, in mid-March, a State Department spokesman announced that I had been recalled for consultations following an "entirely unacceptable" statement of Amin's regarding the U.S. position in Vietnam. This announcement came a month after I had returned to Washington. Our efforts to have Amin's ongoing genocide serve as the main reason for our withdrawal from Uganda were unsuccessful.

Although the same State Department spokesman said that no decision had been made as to when I would return, the prospects were dim. Within a week Margaret began to prepare for her departure in April.

I remained in Washington as an ambassador but I was temporarily assigned to the Department of State. I continued to push for total withdrawal of the official American presence which was completed in the fall of 1973. We returned to academic life.

The years between 1973 and 1977 were emotionally difficult for us. We would learn about the torture and death of so many Ugandans. Our attempts to interest organizations, journals, and the media in the plight of suffering Ugandans were generally unsuccessful.

In this same period there were massive international responses to executions in Spain; torture and imprisonments in Chile and Brazil; and arrests in Korea and the Philippines. All of these regrettable actions were minor in comparison to the deliberate genocide being directed by the chief of state of Uganda.

Also in the same period, two countries in Africa—Rhodesia and South Africa—were the scenes of suffering and death. But the violations in Rhodesia and South Africa were dwarfed by the enormity of the holocaust in Uganda.

We are unable to comprehend the silence maintained by so many nations, organizations, and the United Nations toward the suffering of the Ugandan people when at the same time they would attack lesser violations of human rights in other countries.

The record of selective outrage practiced by so many world leaders makes us fear for the credibility of those countries and organizations dedicated to human rights.

But this unhappy record began to change in early 1977.

Idi Amin is finally being recognized as a brutal tyrant—responsible for the torture and death of untold thousands of his countrymen.

Now it remains for the world community to do something about this tragedy.

Is Idi Amin another Hitler?

2: THE BRUTAL TYRANT EMERGES

WE WENT TO UGANDA EXPECTING TO FIND AN AUTHORITARIAN erratic government, one which we already had doubts about supporting with United States technical assistance and loan programs. Nevertheless, we wanted to see the situation before making a final judgment. We had no idea then, nor did our government, that the extreme brutality and gross perversion of facts, such as occurred in the Stroh-Siedle case, were not just isolated incidents but rather symptoms of a pattern of behavior of Amin's regime which was to grow to astounding proportions.

We had met and worked with military rulers before in Africa. The reality is that throughout the world military governments are increasing in numbers, especially in the Third World. These governments, which do not have the individual protections of a parliamentary society, are authoritarian, but not necessarily brutal.

My first personal meeting with Amin was on July 30, 1972, when my credentials were presented to the President. It was clear that Amin truly loved being on stage. The entire interview was televised. This would not have been unusual if the meeting had been pure diplomatic ceremony with the usual exchanges of courtesies. But it was not. Amin launched into a monologue on U.S.-Ugandan relations with a biting criticism of U.S. policy in Vietnam and other parts of the world.

"The Americans have been defeated in Vietnam but they cannot accept this," he said. "It is very shameful for a superpower like America to fight a small country like North Vietnam." He went on to criticize the U.S. for maintaining military bases in Africa and warned that the CIA was not to operate in Uganda. From my debate training I knew that this first meeting with him was not the place for an argument. I stated the U.S. point of view in clear and succinct terms. The General, however, responded by changing the subject. It was almost as if he did not even hear what I had to say.

Amin then asked for the exact number of Americans living in Uganda and warned about tourists visiting remote villages: "This is very dangerous because some bad people may harm them and

7

then say that General Amin's government has done it." His eyes rolled and his hands danced in front of the television cameras. He went on quickly to two other points—complaining of the U.S. attitude toward Uganda at the International Coffee Organization conference in London in 1971 and warning that certain Israelis had been coming to Uganda on U.S. passports.

I assured him that this was not so, but the General ended the interview by stating, "When I point out the bad things done by Americans, it does not mean that I do not like them."

That evening we sat dumbfounded before our TV watching the daily news program. It normally lasted about two hours, consisting of the same twenty-minute report repeated in six or seven languages. The broadcast of the presentations of my diplomatic credentials was ludicrous. The only person shown speaking was General Amin. The only shots of me were ones when I was listening dutifully to the General. The commentator gave a word-for-word report only of what Amin had said. In closing, I was quoted as having thanked Amin for the warm welcome, expressing the hope that the U.S. would continue its good relations with Uganda.

The Uganda newspaper the next day carried the headline, "President Welcomes New U.S. Ambassador." But a Spanish newspaper was more accurate. "Humiliating Chiding by President of Uganda of New U.S. Ambassador," was the title of an article which lauded "el señor Melady" for having the patience of Job.

It was a masterful piece of propaganda for Idi Amin—the first of many. On the radio and TV, and in the newspapers, Amin stood tall before his people. He had succeeded in scolding the U.S. ambassador who appeared not to have even whimpered. To Uganda's common people, Amin had the courage to attack a major power whose representative was pictured as capitulating before their great Ugandan chief.

It was such a mockery that we laughed. Actually there was nothing that we could do but maintain our sense of humor. Amin had made a clever joke out of the meeting, and we were the butt of it. That was, however, the last time we would ever again laugh at his antics.

Idi Amin started out as a young boy with a tenuous family relationship. He probably did not know who his real father was, and if he did, it is not likely that he saw him very often. Amin's formal education consisted of intermittent attendance at a missionary school. Many have poked fun at Amin, saying that he has a very low intelligence level, but in action he is very clever. He has an unschooled shrewdness, a canny sense of timing, and a primitive art for words. He has less than a sixth-grade level of English and is not embarrassed about it.

Much is still unknown about Amin's life before he became a soldier. He is believed to have been born in 1925, but no birth records exist. In fact, he himself has revealed only fragments about his boyhood, claiming that he came from a poor family where he helped herd goats, carry water, and till the soil to earn money for his parents. But these stories or reminiscences are part of the fictitious drama that Amin often weaves to portray himself as being close to the poverty of the people.

In 1946, he joined the King's African Rifles, an African unit of the British Armed Forces. Evidently, a recruiting party had been sent to northern Uganda to enlist members of the Kakwa (Amin's tribe) into a battalion that was stationed in Langata Camp outside of Nairobi. As in many societies, those who could not obtain an education gravitated to the army where a salary in cash could be earned. In this case, soldiering was a much better alternative to scratching the earth with primitive tools to seek out a day-to-day existence.

Amin's size (230 pounds) and height (six feet three inches) made him stand out among the other recruits. Strong and daring, he became known for his ferocity in carrying out the orders of his commanders. No one thought to give these recruits a political education. They were not expected to think about what they were fighting for—only to fight, and to fight well. Swahili was the *lingua franca* of all the East African services, and particularly the army. In many cases the Swahili language still remains the main language of communication between various African tribes in East Africa. From the point of view of British officers, a private need only know Swahili, but the rank of sergeant required at least the knowledge of simple English.

9

Amin went with the Uganda battalion to Somalia, Northern Uganda, and Kenya. (Frequently he boasts that he served with the British in Burma, but this is highly unreliable since he joined the army after World War II ended.) He served under British Major A. E. D. Mitchell during the suppression of the Mau Mau uprisings in 1952 and 1954. Supposedly he could not be promoted to sergeant because he failed to pass the simple English examination. Finally, after studying the necessary words, he succeeded. In 1957 he was selected to attend an "effendi" course. Effendi was a rank originally invented by the Turkish but used by the British to designate an African rank higher than a noncommissioned officer, but not quite on the same scale as a British commissioned officer. Amin and another officer, Shabani Opoloto, a rival of Amin's, were chosen to be promoted to second lieutenant. The British made a decision to grant independence to Uganda, and they embarked on a crash program to prepare Ugandan officers. In 1961, Amin served under the British officer Hugh Rodgers in the Ugandan Northern Frontier district working to stop cattle raiders.

From the time he entered the army up until Ugandan independence, Amin had been building a reputation as a conscientious soldier. He enthusiastically carried out orders. He mirrored his British officers and impressed his commanders with his zeal. Where others were half asleep, Amin was alert; while his comrades were slovenly, he was stiffly starched and polished. He excelled as a marksman and had remarkable eyesight. Several of his commanding officers have described him as well mannered, respectful, and loyal—a splendid and reliable soldier. Besides, he was cheerful and energetic. He was known to have a remarkable sense of humor and often, when caught in a tight spot, he would answer in a quick and humorous way that would send the British officers away snickering in amusement.

Amin often tells the story that once when he was keeping two wives in his quarters instead of the one allowed by regulation, he explained to an inquiring British officer that one was his wife and the other his elder sister, or "dada" in Swahili. This, he laughs, is how he received the name Idi Amin Dada.

Amin's physical energies were channeled into rugby, swimming, and boxing. He won the light heavyweight championship in Uganda and kept the boxing title for nine years. He enjoys being lauded for his physical prowess. An often repeated news clip portrays Amin at a hotel swimming pool challenging a few young African swimmers to a race. During the race his huge bulk zigzags back and forth interfering with the routes of the other swimmers so that he finishes as the winner. As he emerges from the water, he grins proclaiming himself the best swimmer, and his contesters laugh along with him.

A Ugandan who knew and worked under Amin once told us, "Amin is all soldier constantly at war, and very rarely does he act as a man. He is good at waging wars against individuals, groups, countries, and even against institutions, and fights them successfully to the end." Often critics call Amin insane—he is congenial and amusing, while at the same time he carries on an unending series of torture and killing. This same Ugandan, however, states that this is the ordinary behavior for someone at war. "During war, most bizarre behavior is not only tolerated but accepted as normal."

The British soldiers would laugh when Amin would joke about some infraction of the code or law. He was a rough and tough soldier and that was all that was necessary in the army ranks. As an officer, he continued to squeeze out of tight situations. As a tyrannical leader of his country, he still twists phrases and clowns before the world so that people will laugh rather than cry over the more than one hundred thousand lives he has cruelly taken.

In reading reports of Amin's army record, we can see that his brutality did not emerge overnight. Early in his career, he was accused of being overzealous in his campaign to disarm the cattle rustling members of the Karamajong tribe. He was very successful but his methods were harsh.

Once, while on duty at the border area between Northern Uganda and Kenya, Amin was implicated in the killing of three Turkana tribesmen. His company had been ordered to disarm the tribesmen, who were believed to be engaged in cattle rustling. Amin was then a lieutenant and in charge of one of the platoons. After his platoon had raided one of the villages and returned with the guns, a number of the Turkana tribesmen complained that

11

several of their members had been murdered. An investigation was carried out by the army, but a court-martial never took place.

The deposed President Milton Obote, who was prime minister from 1962 to 1966 and president from 1967 to 1971, claimed that the British governor informed him of the case against Amin. It had been recommended that Amin be dismissed since the evidence was clearly against him. However, Obote states that he thwarted the court-martial since Amin was one of only two army officers that Uganda would have at independence. He recommended only a severe reprimand. "I regret to say that part of Uganda's present suffering, sickness, and inhumanity can be traced to the opinion I gave to Sir Walter," Obote later stated.

By the time of Ugandan independence, Idi Amin had risen from a simple, barely educated recruit in the King's African Rifles to a major in the Uganda army of one thousand men with about forty British officers. Amin had become familiar with army organization and commands and had learned the rudiments of the English language. Most of all, he had learned to be a vicious soldier. He had been rewarded for his bloodthirsty actions, obtaining promotions from his British commanders who considered him an effective military leader. One of his British commanders described Amin as a natural sergeant—but not more than that. He followed orders well, he was tough and energetic, and he could rally men to follow him into a foray or battle. But as an army commander, he would have to devise and give the commands, to deliberate the consequences, and to make decisions based on reason and purpose for army actions. A few men have been successful at rising through the ranks and becoming responsible military commanders despite the fact that they had no formal officer training.

For Amin the military represented the only course for upward mobility. Curiously enough, this did not seem to be behind Amin's persistent rise in the armed forces. He was clearly in love with the military. He relished his duties and thoroughly enjoyed every little detail. Life as a civilian in the northwestern region of Uganda had been monotonous and unrewarding. As a soldier, Amin tasted the glamour of serving abroad—in Somalia and Kenya. The duties he was assigned—such as disarming cattle rustlers and keeping vigil against raiding Mau Mau insurgents—were exciting and competitive games.

Amin fared well under the colonial system because he mimicked his British officers and earned the reputation of being a respectful soldier. He was no revolutionary.

Amin delighted in military parades, military uniforms, and the carrying of the colors. To this day he is fascinated with military dress and sports many different varieties of combat and dress attire. Many men have succumbed to the fascination of military pomp, but few have relished actual combat. Amin, however, was always eager to participate in forays. Even now, Amin relishes a fight. He offered the services of his soldiers to help crush the Israelis. He promised to send his troops to Zaïre to assist President Mobutu in his clash with Katanga dissidents. He explained that he took the title Field Marshal in order to lead the victorious liberation of southern Africa.

His triumphs as a young army soldier were often attributed to his cruel and harsh means. Some contend that war breeds evil. Those who are forced to kill often end up relishing the very act of cruelty. In the United States, Americans were shocked when the details of the My Lai Massacres in Vietnam were released. Few thought that American soldiers could be capable of such horrible deeds. The actions were due to combat fatigue, many claimed. The men were believed to have gone berserk. The fact was that evil had become routine. It was accepted, especially when inflicted on Vietnamese victims—people of another race.

In the colonial army, the British often recruited soldiers among the more disadvantaged ethnic groups. First, because a number of people from remote areas were attracted to the military. Second, since they were less educated, they made good followers who accepted without question orders given by the British officers. And finally, they were accustomed to a rough and sometimes dangerous life. In many cases, soldiers were employed to police sections of the country outside of the area of their own tribes. Thus, Amin (a Kakwa) was not employed in the West Nile section. He was sent on operations against the Karamajong in Uganda and the Turkana tribe and the Mau Mau in Kenya. At other times he was stationed in Jinja, a stronghold of the Basoga people. He learned to stuff handkerchiefs down the throats of Kenyans and threaten to cut the penises of Turkana tribesmen—all striking similarities between the My Lai carnage in Vietnam and the tribal massacres ordered by Amin. Both acts of cruelty were carried out under military orders. Both contained elements of bitter racism.

Idi Amin learned to imitate well the different aspects and actions of personalities which appealed to him. He acquired the trappings of a professional soldier, but he performed his duty without acquiring a sense of duty. In other words, he imitated the externals while remaining uncommitted to any ideal.

During our nine months in Uganda, we noticed what a sharp eye Amin had for details. While visiting another country, if something appealed to him—a new piece of military equipment, a ceremony, or a different form of combat unit—he would immediately acquire or institute these new things on arrival back home in Uganda. During the visit of President (now Emperor) Bokassa of the Central African Republic (now Empire), Amin continually admired Bokassa's wide and regal ribbons covered with heavy medals from shoulder to hip. Bokassa was such a small man that he could hardly stand at attention under the weight of so many distinctions. A few days later, Amin appeared at another ceremony with ribbons and medals neatly arranged. However, the weight of these sundry medals, many of which Amin had conferred upon himself, did not bother at all the huge frame of the hefty field marshal. Another time, President Mobutu of Zaïre arrived at Entebbe's airport with an African chief's staff. Again, Amin had a similar staff within a few days.

During the British colonial days, and shortly thereafter, Amin imitated his British officer friends well—with one very real difference. He had no sense of honor or loyalty to a civilian government as did those who served in the Queen's Service. He was of peasant stock from a remote area of Uganda. He had not been schooled in the political distinctions between the government of the people and the duty of the military to those people.

In the early period of independence, Amin remained a loyal soldier in an army commanded by British officers. The honeymoon did not last long, Amin and his closest rival, Shabani

14

Opoloto, had attained the rank of effendi—the highest rank that most Africans could attain in the British army. At independence, when the King's African Rifles was transformed into the Uganda Rifles, both Amin and Opoloto became commissioned officers. In 1964, a revolution in Zanzibar occurred which sparked mutinies in the Kenyan and Tanzanian armies. Quickly it spread to the Ugandan army barracks in Jinja. The soldiers wanted to oust the British officers and were demanding more pay. Essentially they won. Pay revisions boosted salaries of the formerly ill-paid soldiers, making their profession one of the most remunerative in the country. The Uganda government headed by Milton Obote asked many of the British officers to leave, promoted Amin and Opoloto to lieutenant colonel, and gave each of them command over a battalion.

Amin had quickly evolved from soldier to army commander. He soon became aware of the fact that he had some political cards to play. No longer were the British in control. He had to contend with his fellow Ugandans who now controlled the government. Faced with the fact that he had a rival for the top commanding post in Shabani Opoloto, Amin threw his support to Prime Minister Obote when the Baganda (the people of Buganda) formulated plans to oust the prime minister.

In 1966 Amin led the army on an attack of the king's palace in Buganda, forcing the *kabaka* or king to flee into exile in Britain. The attack was bloody with several hundred killed. But because of it, Obote owed Amin a favor. Despite an impending charge of embezzlement that implicated Amin in the gold and ivory trade with Congo nationalists, Amin was promoted by Obote to army chief of staff. His rival, Opoloto, because of his Buganda links, was isolated into another position. Amin came out on top through his merciless attack on the king's palace. He had given his support to a prime minister whom he ousted less than five years afterward. In the course of that five-year period, Amin began to long for absolute power. He now knew the satisfaction of giving commands and having a large contingent blindly obey. He had had his first taste of that power, and it appealed to him.

For those five years under Obote as army chief of staff, he concentrated on building a sizable army, spending vast amounts on equipment and ammunition. Just before his overthrow, Obote demanded an explanation from Amin of the huge overexpenditures for defense. Amin never accounted for it.

Amin had emerged as an astute and cunning politician. He had joined forces with a man he eventually plotted against to consolidate his position. He gradually built up the number of northern army recruits, especially from his West Nile region, a region already making up a sizable part of the Ugandan army. The money spent for defense was indeed mismanaged and it was quite probable that much of it went to securing allies for his eventual struggle to take over the government.

Some British sources have claimed that Amin financed many of the southern Sudanese forces who were at the time engaged in a struggle against the Sudanese government. While this conflict has been resolved, Ugandans continually claim that southern Sudanese soldiers have now been integrated into the Ugandan army to shore up Amin's power base. Refugees from Uganda continue to claim that Sudanese soldiers roam the Ugandan countryside terrorizing the population.

Shortly after we arrived, we saw that Amin had an unusual desire to be at the center of the stage. He enjoyed the mere giving of orders for the sake of having them followed, and delighted in having the entire country lean on his every word. The presence of TV cameras, as during the presentation of my credentials, was an everyday occurrence. Each day, the front page of the government-controlled newspaper, *Voice of Uganda*, carried pictures and statements from General Amin. The television news carried verbatim reports of his speeches, pronouncements, and indeed his many off-the-cuff remarks which more than once were picked up by the international news media.

Amin is consumed by power. A part of his game is to appear to be on the same level as, or above, world leaders. Thus, he is in the habit of firing off testy telegrams to presidents and monarchs throughout the world. He gives his opinions and expects them to be fully accepted by other heads of state on the affairs of their particular countries. To him it is quite natural. Amin sees his power as extending far beyond the country of Uganda.

What he has done, and is continuing to do within the Ugandan

16

borders, is atrocious, but being consumed by his own power, he would not hesitate to extend those atrocities outside his borders to his neighbors and beyond. Defiantly and tempestuously he has said, "I do not want to be controlled by any superpower. I myself consider myself the most powerful figure in the world and that is why I do not let any superpower control me."

Some pass such a statement off as being ludicrous and silly. How could someone like Idi Amin, ruler of a small nation such as Uganda, be a threat to a superpower? We saw first-hand how Amin can play havoc with the citizens of other countries. We have seen, too, how he mistreats his own compatriots. The only ludicrous aspect of such a statement is that often Amin ends up doing just what he says.

For that brief moment we had laughed over Amin and his silly antics during the presentation of my credentials. Thereafter, we knew to take him seriously.

The world—fed by international press and media—has laughed too. In 1974 a French-made film shown in Western Europe and America made audiences howl with laughter. The director of the film, Barbet Schroeder, remarked, "I let him speak for himself; he comes across exactly the way he is. You get the feeling that he's totally crazy." When the film was shown in Britain, London critics commented that Amin was "the funniest actor since Woody Allen" and that the film was "a masterpiece of unconscious comedy." Amin quickly protested to the film's producer and demanded that certain scenes be cut. The French filmmaker gave in and dropped several scenes including the filming of an execution.

The portrayal of the big oversized dictator with his stiff but colorful English speech was an amusing character sketch. The sad fact is that he is real—not fictitious—and what he says is not uttered in fun, but in dead seriousness.

Amin has been described by many as having a light and entertaining side. We saw him, on occasion, join the traditional dancers for a round of hip-swinging dances. He would bring out his accordion and play a few tunes. He plays with little children and takes one of his young sons along everywhere he goes. (We were told that a sorcerer once warned Amin that he would risk assassination if he did not bring along one of his younger sons.) On

17

every plane trip that Amin takes, one of his sons appears with him, usually dressed in army fatigues. The boy, four or five years old, mimics his father in a salute and sometimes is given a rifle to carry.

Amin still enjoys the comradery of military life. He frequently visits the barracks for a beer and a round of crude jokes. The men are flattered by Amin's ability to fraternize with them. To keep the military happy, he showers soldiers with luxuries not available to the average Ugandan. Fancy clothes and expensive watches are imported from Europe to pay for the loyalty of his personal guards and security force. When other Ugandans have to line up to receive rations of sugar and salt, the soldiers and their families have ample supplies.

To many soldiers, the army has quickly brought the good life to them. Amin is, therefore, their savior and protector. The hard-core groups responsible for his protection and his dirty work are particularly loyal to him; for if anything happens to Amin, they, too, will suffer. To solidify the savior image, Amin often colors his remarks to his troops with friendly, fatherly advice. He exhorts them to lead clean lives, being vigilant against gonorrhea, and warns them about hoarding foodstuffs bound for the ordinary people.

Amin has woven his rule with an aura of spirituality. Suddenly after becoming the "top man," he began claiming his Moslem heritage. This was particularly apparent after he visited Colonel Qaddafi, the military ruler of Libya, and subsequently threw out the Israelis. He started visiting mosques and encouraging Moslem organizations.

Many times while we were in Uganda, Amin visited the Christian communities to assure them that although he was a devout Moslem, he in no way would interfere with the religion of Christians. During a meeting of Catholic church leaders, Amin presented himself at the Catholic mass, taking a seat in the sanctuary. He guaranteed all present that he had great respect for the three main religions in Uganda—Catholic, Protestant, and Moslem.

He frequently uses God in his speech, giving the impression to the simple, believing Ugandan that he is a prophet. Indeed, Amin

18

often tells the story that in 1952, he had a dream that told how he would lead the army and the people. When he announced his expulsion of the Asians in 1972, he claimed that God had told him to do so in a dream. He was asked by a reporter if he dreams very often and he answered in dead seriousness, "Only when it is necessary."

It is necessary to build himself up in the eyes of the average Ugandan as someone who is destined to rule. Many Ugandans still hold to the old traditions and superstitions of the past. Some, even though highly educated, still believe in witchcraft. Amin realizes this, for he himself is fascinated with the spirits. His own mother was said to have earned a living by practicing witchcraft. Seers and spiritualists from other parts of Africa frequently come to Uganda to foretell Amin's future.

Amin, the self-proclaimed prophet, exhorts his people to be more religious and to believe in God. At the same time, he carries on a constant war against the Christian communities in Uganda. His battle against the Christians is not necessarily a result of his Moslem faith. It is merely a lashing out at any group or institution which might pose some threat to his regime.

Amin's sense of humor is sadistic. Most of what was generally laughed at by diplomats and other foreigners in Kampala were genuinely serious statements and actions of Amin. However, at times, we noticed that Amin deliberately used sarcasm to mock his critics. Those he decided to punish would be brought meekly to the cruel tyrant who would force them to make fools of themselves. He would smile in a sadistic way, knowing full well that after having made them a laughingstock he would have them killed and thrown to the crocodiles.

Amin especially enjoys making fun of the British. Turning the tables on them is a clever and amusing pastime to him. Who can forget the photo of a group of European businessmen carrying Amin in a sedan chair? Another time, he insisted that the Europeans kneel to take an oath of allegiance to Amin. "In the future, any British citizen who wants to see me must kneel before me as [the] Baganda used to kneel before the British," he proclaimed. To those millions of Baganda people who had suffered under colonial rule, he was a genius to invent such a sport. The Africans delighted in his game, for at last they could needle their former colonial masters and have fun at the same time.

To the Asians who had secured their Ugandan citizenship and stayed behind after all others were expelled, Amin announced that they would have the honor of living in the countryside and farming. He knew it would frighten the brown-skinned men and boys who stood before him, for they had never been farmers and had no intention of moving to the remote areas. But Amin delighted in his little joke.

Idi Amin is obviously not a scholar of history. His ability to read English or any language is unknown. Most of his knowledge of past events has been gleaned from oral reports and movies. Yet unconsciously, his actions, motives, and methods are reminiscent of past tyrannies and common to many brutal dictators.

Napoleon was an exceedingly capable writer in describing his glorious and exaggerated part in battle. Amin, despite his shaky knowledge of English, also has an uncanny sense of color and humor when it comes to portraying himself as the hero in Africa. Many evil men and women have been capable of expressing warmth and even love at the same time they are carrying on brutal and despicable acts. Not too long ago, millions read the book and viewed the motion picture *The Godfather*, in which the warmth and devotion toward the family of the gangster figure was intertwined with the harsh and brutal life of a criminal.

Amin uses the word "love" in his pronouncements, and although sometimes sarcastically, hints of his genuine affection. Among the people he has claimed to "love" are President Julius Nyerere of Tanzania, President Carter, the American people, and, of course, the British. With the British, he has been particularly consistent in his assurance of his affection. While we were in Uganda, he asked the British High Commissioner Slater to leave after a dispute over the Asian expulsion, but at the same time insisted on his friendship with the British people. He sent a mission to Britain which carried his message that Uganda and Britain were of the same family and that occasionally there are arguments between brothers. He has a nostalgic affection for his British army experience and still maintains contact with some of his former commanders.

Whenever there is a flaring of tempers between the two countries, Amin reassures his "friends" that his argument is only with British politicians. But Amin's love-hate relationship continues with the British. He assured the British that he would attend the Commonwealth meeting which coincided with the celebration of the twenty-fifth anniversary of the queen's reign in 1977. The British, on the other hand, desperately hoped that they would be spared this embarrassment. They were spared but only after many threats.

Curiously, Amin also maintains a friendly relationship with a former Israeli officer, Colonel Bar-Lev, who was said to be his confidant when he toppled President Obote. During the Israeli attack on Uganda's airport to free the hostages held from the hijacked Air France plane, the Israelis used Colonel Bar-Lev to make contact with General Amin.

It is quite natural for soldiers to make good friends during their military service. Army buddies remain affectionate friends despite years and miles of drifting apart. Amin is no exception. The military was his world and he excelled in it. He remembers those who helped him to achieve success.

Amin took over in January 1971. All reports that we read after my appointment in 1972 clearly indicated that he was an authoritarian military ruler. In this regard, he joined many such rulers in this category who, since 1960, have been increasing in numbers.

Before leaving Washington for Uganda, we had read about Amin's background. I had been briefed on his occasional erratic behavior. Since Amin had seized the presidency of Uganda, there was one ugly incident involving Americans which vividly portrayed his murderous behavior. This was the killing of Robert L. Siedle and Nicholas Stroh in July 1971.

The embassy's files were thick with the sad and sinister events. Stroh, a freelance journalist who wrote for several U.S. newspapers including the *Washington Star* and the *Philadelphia Bulletin*, had decided to journey to Mbarara to check reports that there had been tribal fighting in the army barracks located in the small Ugandan town. Siedle, a lecturer at the University of Makerere in Kampala, was working on a book about Christian missionary

President Idi Amin is carried by four Britons into official reception, in a makeshift throne. This was Amin's idea—he felt it would show new white man's burden in Africa.

activities in Uganda. He decided to accompany Nicholas Stroh in order to do some research for his book. They both went to the camp to see if they could interview the commanding officer, Lieutenant Colonel Ali, who was in Kampala at the time. They were asked to return the next day.

The following morning Stroh left Siedle in the hotel and headed for the camp. A little while later, several members of Uganda's Special Army Force came to the hotel and took Siedle away with them. No one ever heard anything from the two Americans again.

The U.S. Embassy in Kampala began asking questions of their whereabouts. Getting nowhere, they presumed the two were dead and pressured the Ugandan government into making an inquiry. Amin finally agreed and appointed a judicial commission headed by Justice David Jeffreys-Jones, a British judge who was serving on the Uganda High Court. For months the commission received nothing but conflicting reports and evasive answers.

In April 1972, a young Ugandan army lieutenant, Silver Tibihika, escaped across the border to Tanzania and told of his role in the affair. Relying on Tibihika's description, Justice Jones went to search for Stroh's missing car. He found the wrecked and crushed Volkswagen at the bottom of a deep ravine in the foothills of the Mountains of the Moon in western Uganda. Later Jones obtained a deposition from Tibihika for the commission.

Justice Jones at last had evidence that implicated the Simba battalion at the Mbarara army base in the death of Stroh and Siedle. The commission's report was so devastating that Jones, fearing reprisals, left the country in June 1972 before he sent the report.

Jones had found that two top army officers, Major Juma and Lt. Col. Ali Fadul had been involved in the cover-up. Major Juma had seen the two Americans and knew that they had been killed. Stroh had been seen in the camp by the young army Lieutenant Tibihika, who had overheard accounts by other soldiers that the journalist had argued with Major Juma. The soldiers had boasted about how they had killed the two Americans and described jokingly the last words of Stroh, "You will answer for this one day." After Lt. Colonel Ali had returned from Kampala,

Tibihika was taken to the place where Stroh and Siedle had been buried. He was ordered to dig up the remains, place them in sacks, and transport them back to the barracks where the bodies were burned and the ashes thrown into the river. The car was likewise burned and thrown over a cliff. According to Tibihika's report, the two men had been killed at knife point.

The military authorities were sure that all evidence had been destroyed, but Jones had unearthed the fact that Nicholas Stroh and Robert Siedle had indeed been murdered by members of the Simba battalion of the Uganda armed forces.

Amin, on receiving the report, was angry that Jones had mailed the report from outside Uganda. He then issued a White Paper—the official government statement—declaring that the two Americans had met their deaths somewhere in Mbarara at the hands of unidentified persons!

The commission report and the White Paper had been made public just before our arrival in Kampala. Some in the State Department had grown impatient with the long and tedious negotiations. They were somewhat relieved that at least some satisfaction regarding the deaths had been obtained. There is a tendency for large organizations to treat such tragedies as minor incidents in view of much broader goals. In the case of the murders of Stroh and Siedle, it was the determination of Mrs. Nicholas Stroh, his widow, and his family which at least brought the Jones report to the public.

Amin later paid both the Stroh and Siedle families compensation, but he never lifted a finger to prosecute those who had been implicated in the murders and cover-up. The whole affair had been dismissed just as if it had never happened. The murderers are still free. One day they should be brought to justice; it is doubtful that they ever will under the Amin regime.

With my ambassadorial appointment to Uganda, the atmosphere in the U.S. Embassy was that the Stroh-Siedle problem had been solved and the way was now clear for another ambassador to start afresh with General Amin. Officially, our government did not want to acknowledge the stark probability that Amin had orchestrated a cover-up of the murders of the two Americans. In the spring of 1972, it was difficult to find anyone in the U.S.

government who would classify Amin as a murderous tyrant. However, in June 1977, a well-known and highly respected Ugandan leader in exile told us that the orders for the killings of Stroh and Siedle came directly from Amin.

The growing fear in our hearts, starting within ninety days of our arrival, was that Amin was looming on the scene of world leaders as a confirmed brutal tyrant practicing torture and murder.

3: THE BRUTAL TYRANT IN ACTION

THE UGANDAN PEOPLE LIVE IN FEAR.

Day after day come reports of disappearances, arrests, torture, and brutal killings carried out by members of Amin's special killer squads. The police are powerless to do anything. There is no safety in the country. No one is immune from the whims of the soldiers.

In the beginning, those who had been associated with the former President Obote by profession or tribe were listed for elimination. Then, those of certain other tribes with an education were marked. Now, even the barely literate peasant is harassed and hunted by Amin's henchmen.

The International Commission of Jurists published its report on Uganda in 1977. This distinguished nongovernmental lawyers' organization has, over a twenty-five-year period, established a reputation for objectivity and impartiality. In its recent report on Uganda, the commission conservatively estimates that the number of victims of Amin's brutal reign of terror has passed the 100,000 mark. We know that the number is much greater because many people, and even entire families, will never be accounted for.

There are those who have escaped; but now they must live with scenes of horror for the rest of their lives. They tell of bodies floating in the Nile River, of bones scattered in the forests and hanging from trees. The once magnificent beauty of the country of Uganda has been defiled by the bloody and diabolic rule of Idi Amin. Many of the gruesome and brutal tortures and murders have been carried out under direct orders from Amin. Many other cruel killings have been done by officers and soldiers of the Public Safety Unit and the Bureau of State Research—units of the police and army that Amin specifically uses for the sole purpose of carrying out the task of elimination. The tyranny continues, and with each death and torture, the regime slips further and further into the depths of hell.

The evil practiced by Amin and those associated with him in these endless crimes only breeds more and more evil. The cancer continues to grow to obscene proportions. The tale of the Amin regime reads like a fictitious horror story. If we had not been there and had not known both those who escaped and those who were victims of such horror, perhaps we, too, would have believed that the reports were exaggerated and unobjective. If anything, the reports of those who saw and experienced the suffering are just a fraction of what has really occurred in Uganda; for the full evidence of the cruelty rests in the silent and decaying bodies lying in the remote forests and swamps of Uganda.

We had been to Uganda several times before we arrived on diplomatic assignment in 1972. Uganda had held a special fascination for us. It was this unique feeling for Uganda that influenced our decision to leave Bujumbura, Burundi for Kampala. I had served as U.S. ambassador to Burundi since 1969. When discussion arose in the State Department regarding my next assignment, two other countries in Africa were presented besides Uganda. The first proposal would have required our leaving Burundi earlier, so we declined. We wanted to complete a normal tour of duty, about two years, and to avoid interrupting our children's education in mid-year.

The other offer, a French-speaking country in West Africa, was submitted with Uganda and we had to make a choice. (The previous U.S. ambassador to Uganda, Dr. Clyde Ferguson, had been reassigned to the State Department in Washington.) It should have been a difficult choice, for both areas were attractive in terms of climate, culture, and people. However, Uganda for us was special. So despite the appearance that it would not be an easy assignment, I chose Kampala.

The country of Uganda was a favorite African attraction for many people because of its excellent climate, its beautiful countryside, its kingdoms with their long history, its wealth of wild animals, and the special flavor of its capital, Kampala, built, like Rome, on seven hills.

For us it was all of these things and more. Uganda had a special place in our lives, for it was through Ugandan friends that we first met each other in 1960. These friends had studied in the United States and had since returned to their country. As we prepared to arrive, we grew anxious to see these friends with whom we had remained in contact more than ten years.

When our plane touched down at Entebbe airport in Uganda, it was early morning. The mist from Lake Victoria was clearing as the heat of the day began to soak up the moisture from the swamp grasslands bordering the lake. Members of the U.S. Embassy in Kampala, Uganda, were on hand to greet us as well as officials from the Uganda protocol office. (The embassy in Kampala had a medium-sized staff of 13 Americans, augmented by 106 Peace Corps members, 21 members of a mission of the Agency for International Development, 3 members of the U.S. Information Agency, and a U.S. Marine detachment of 5.)

As we walked through the group at the airport we noticed an African priest, Father Clement Kiggundu, who was then editor of *Munno*, the only Catholic daily in Africa. Two years previously, Father Kiggundu had appeared at my office in New York when I was serving at the U.S. Mission to the United Nations. He had asked for advice on studying journalism in the United States. Knowing of a program at my alma mater, I arranged for him to visit Duquesne University in Pittsburgh, where he subsequently spent two years studying journalism and working for the *Pittsburgh Catholic*.

Father Kiggundu was extremely enthusiastic about seeing us, and we were equally pleased. Not often is one able to see the successful results of a project to which one has given a little help along the way. We had no idea at the time that Father Kiggundu had only a few months to live.

In January 1973, Father Clement Kiggundu was found dead in a burned car on the road from Kampala to Jinja. The government tried to pass off his death as an automobile accident, since the Jinja road was notoriously dangerous for motorists. However, an autopsy was performed and the results, publicly announced from the pulpit of the Rubaga Cathedral, confirmed that the priest had been found shot. Subsequently, the doctor who had performed the autopsy disappeared as well.

We were shocked not only by the ruthless killing, but by the bold and crude methods which the government used to deceive the people. We had only known Father Kiggundu a short time but we were impressed by his competence. It was a difficult enough task to be committed to accurate reporting without incurring the wrath of Amin. Kiggundu evidently became too much of a threat to Amin when he decided to publish a report on a women's conference that had taken place in Kampala in November. At this meeting the women called for an investigation of the disappearances of innocent people and criticized the Ugandan government for not controlling the continued violence in the country.

The massive bloodletting that occurred in Uganda involved other very good friends of ours whom we had known as students in New York in the early sixties.

The fate of Joseph Mubiru was a particularly personal tragedy for both of us, for Joe had in fact introduced us to each other at an international student meeting in New York in 1960.

On the morning of our arrival in Kampala in July 1972, a message of welcome from Joe was waiting for us at our residence. We planned a reunion dinner with the Mubirus and some other friends for the next week.

At the dinner, all were cautiously critical of Amin. Their main criticisms fell into two categories—Amin's refusal to take advice from technocrats on the running of systematic government, and the fear that there would be an anti-Christian movement. Joe Mubiru had served as governor of the National Bank of Uganda under President Obote. Mubiru continued at the bank after Amin's coup in 1971, until Joe's fiscal policies began to be thwarted by the erratic decisions and actions of Amin and his top people. Amin criticized Mubiru, and Joe answered by publicly printing a rebuttal to the criticism along with his resignation. Mubiru then decided to leave politics completely and go into business. He was doing private consulting at the time we arrived.

To us as Americans, accustomed to a parliamentary democracy, Joe Mubiru's posture was a normal and everyday occurrence. He recognized that he was not in power, but believed he had the right to mildly criticize Amin or defend his own policies. He hoped that by making his criticism public—and indeed this criticism was merely on financial policy—he would be able to avoid being suspected of secretive plotting. However, we knew that in many developing societies today free and open criticism is impossible. Even the relatively insignificant criticism of Joe Mubiru would not go unnoticed by Amin, who would be continually suspicious of Mubiru's independence and following.

We probably would not have been at all surprised if Joe had been arrested or detained under house arrest by Amin, but instead he was brutally murdered.

Joe Mubiru's fear of action against Christians particularly interested us, but we were not willing to take it seriously enough at the time. Amin had already thrown out the Israelis and had begun an anti-Zionist line similar to that of his new patron, Colonel Qaddafi of Libya. Amin had also emphasized his Moslem religion, but up to this point had not attacked the Christians. In fact, he seemed to go out of his way to show his support for religion in general and encourage all the faiths.

Joe Mubiru was also a member of the Baganda tribe. Christians in Buganda experienced bitter and cruel purges carried out by their *kabaka* or king in the nineteenth century. The Baganda were heavily Christian now. We thought that maybe Joe's fears were exaggerated and unfounded.

The last time we saw Joe Mubiru alive was in the office of Emmanuel Nsubuga, the Catholic Archbishop of Kampala. We had gone there to make a standard courtesy call. Joe Mubiru had just finished a fund-raising meeting for the Catholic newspaper. We had not made contact with him for some time. A few days previously, I had been warned privately by a Ugandan government official that it would be dangerous for us to continue seeing Joe Mubiru and some of our other old friends who had studied in the United States.

As we greeted Joe briefly that day, Margaret lingered behind a few minutes to convey to Joe the difficulty we had in seeing him and to somehow warn him of possible trouble. There was an immediate understanding on Joe's part. He had always been highly politicized, but now he appeared resolute and perhaps foolishly courageous. Only a few weeks passed after that meeting when news reached us of Joe's disappearance. Somehow we vainly hoped that Joe had really disappeared and would show up at some time outside of the country.

It was useless. There was no doubt that he, along with others, had been killed. Only months afterward did we know the full horror of how Joe met his death.

Before Joe had been arrested, Amin had threatened that he

would be detained under cold water—this referred to a method of torture in which the victim is held under cold water for hours. Mubiru was taken to Makindye Military Police Barracks located just outside of Kampala along with many others who disappeared at the time. While we do not know the full details of how he finally met his death, we know some of the cruel methods used on others in the same prison. Amin's threats have often been carried out. It would not be surprising if he had ordered his threat to be carried out on Joe Mubiru.

No chance was even given to have a decent funeral for Joe. No one dared to have a memorial service. His wife and children left the city and went into hiding.

We were both sickened by Joe Mubiru's death. His murder represented such a waste of time, effort, money, and determination to build competent technicians in Africa. For Margaret it was a deep personal loss. She looked back on college days when she first met him. He was a slight, fine-featured man. His glasses were continually slipping down over a nose that was hardly there. From October to May, his black African skin had been wrapped for protection by layers of heavy and oversized woolens.

Joe Mubiru was already thirty years old in 1960 when he met a group of students from the College of New Rochelle, a women's college outside of New York. Margaret recalls how he stood out as a leader among all the others. Almost always, when the conversation turned to politics, Joe would usually monopolize it. He had earned a degree in India before coming to the United States for graduate studies in economics.

Joseph Mubiru was no ordinary man. During his studies for his doctorate he had suffered from a nervous breakdown and was forced to abandon his studies and return to Uganda without the degree. We had worried that he would become bitter over his failure, but instead, in a few short years, he became head of the National Bank of Uganda.

Despite the fact that he was out of the government when he was killed, Joe Mubiru was still contributing in positive ways to the development of Uganda. His death proved a tragic loss for his country and a frightful waste of so many years of effort and training.

31

Father Clement Kiggundu, editor of *Munno*, with Dr. Melady in July 1972. He was murdered several months later.

Joseph Mubiru, who was killed a short time after this photo was taken in October 1972.

The story of Joseph Mubiru illustrates what has happened in Uganda. There are many more like Joe—lawyers, doctors, teachers, students, priests, bishops, and the chief justice—many people who met death at the whim of a cruel tyrant and his henchmen. The country of Uganda has been deprived of the services of many able and dedicated men and women.

When our Ugandan assignment began, we had read of the killings that had already taken place after Amin's coup. We were aware that many political scientists had classified these killings as the usual purge that occurs after a change in power. American, British and French specialists in African affairs believed that things would settle down as soon as Amin consolidated his power.

At his first press conference in January 1971, President Amin contended that the coup that thrust him into power had been bloodless. It was true that it was relatively bloodless for the first few days. But thereafter his regime was marked with blood and violence.

When the coup took place, the army was dominated by soldiers from the Acholi and Lango tribes of northern Uganda. Some estimate that they made up about 40 percent of the military force. President Milton Obote had been a Lango, and many other Ugandan officials had been from the Lango and neighboring Acholi tribes.

In the year that followed, about two-thirds of the Langi and Acholi soldiers in the army were killed. On the very day of Amin's first press announcement, the two army officers who had attempted to counter Amin's coup had been beaten to death. Afterward a pattern of systematic routing-out of the Acholi and Langi from the military occurred. Large groups of these victims were taken to Makindye Military Prison. They were thrown into two notorious cells which were called ''Singapore'' and ''Dar es Salaam'' in reference to the fact that former President Obote was overthrown while attending a conference in Singapore and then took refuge in Dar es Salaam, Tanzania. A witness described the scene when thirty-six officers were brought to the room. Some of them were crawling and crying in pain from broken legs and arms. Three or four soldiers moved into the room and started shooting. After a few minutes, they stopped; and all that could be heard were the groans and screams of the wounded. The bodies were dragged out and those who were still alive were killed with machetes or shot to death. The next morning the witness and several other inmates were given scrubbing brushes and pails and were told to clean up the cell. The blood on the floor was almost a quarter of an inch thick, and pieces of skull bones, teeth, brain tissue, and flesh littered the room where the horrible massacre had taken place. After the first barrage of shootings, the army decided to devise other means of eliminating their prisoners to conserve bullets. A witness tells that forty Acholi and Langi soldiers were taken to the Singapore cell and bayonetted to death. Another reports that bayonets and knives were used to cut throats and behead the prisoners. This went on night after night as more and more Acholi and Langi were brought into the camp. After each killing, the bodies would be loaded on trucks and taken away for burial.

Hundreds of Acholi and Langi soldiers who were based at Mbarara were separated from the other troops and taken to a nearby farm in June 1971. Their throats were slit. Similar incidents occurred throughout Uganda at various military barracks. In Jinja, the violence spread outside the barracks to villages of Acholi families in which even the children were killed.

In the beginning, news of the large-scale massacres of these tribesmen who had formed the nucleus of Obote's political base did not filter out to the people. The Amin government used various means to cover up any suspicious evidence. For example, to explain the killings that took place by the explosion in a military barracks just outside of Kampala, a spokesman for the President's office said that there should be no cause for alarm. The army was destroying a damaged bomb. In effect, thirty-two senior Acholi and Langi officers had been packed into a room at Malire. Explosives were put into the room and detonated, killing all of them.

As the news finally began to leak out to the public, other explanations were used. President Amin suggested that Chinese experts from Tanzania were involved in the outbreaks of violence that had taken place in Uganda. He also charged that there had been border attacks. There had, in fact, been attempts on the part of Milton Obote to launch training camps outside of Uganda, both in Tanzania and in Sudan. The Sudanese venture ended abruptly, when Amin's loyal troops from the Anayana tribes in northern Uganda thwarted a group of Acholi and Langi on their way across the border to Sudan. All were killed by orders of Amin.

The resistance movement in Tanzania, however, continued because Obote was being supported by Tanzanian President Julius Nyerere. During this period, however, the killings of Acholi and Langi soldiers occurred almost exclusively in the military barracks and were carried out by other members of the Ugandan military. Amin, however, used the Obote presence in Tanzania to fool the people into thinking that there had truly been heavy border clashes between Uganda and Obote followers crossing from Tanzania. In truth, only two minor clashes at the border occurred in 1971.

The killings spread to include some civilians and police officers. Michael Kaggwa, president of the Industrial Court, a tribunal to settle labor disputes was tied to the steering wheel of his car which was then burned. Mathias Omuge, formerly of Ugandan television, was driven off in a car with several unidentified men and never seen again.

At the end of December 1971, a large number of police officers, members of the General Services Department (an elite one-thousand-man presidential bodyguard that also gathered intelligence), and the remainder of the Acholi and Langi soldiers were transferred from a civilian prison to the army prison at Mutukula near the Tanzanian border. The prisoners were told they were taken there for a court-martial. In fact, each day a group of them were tied together and taken out to be killed. Some were told to run with their hands tied behind their backs and were shot while running. Out of the more than five hundred marked for death, only a handful escaped to tell the gruesome details of how those who did not die after being shot were beaten on the heads until they died.

In February, Radio Uganda—the government radio station— broadcast a statement from Amin saying that a minor incident had happened at Mutukula in which fifteen remaining detainees had attempted to escape. He told how they fled to Tanzania, were arrested by the Tanzanian Security Forces, and handed back to the Uganda army. Amin expressed his personal gratitude to the Tanzanians at the border for having apprehended the escapees.

People in Uganda were subjected to these lies every day, but gradually the truth filtered to some by word of mouth. The diplomatic community in Kampala, however, in 1971 and 1972 was prepared to excuse these outbursts of violence and killings as an aftermath of a coup.

In 1972, the killings in the military barracks died down. The Acholi and Langi members had been virtually eliminated. The civilian disappearances, however, continued sporadically. William Kalema, minister of commerce and industry under Obote, who had been outside Uganda during the coup, decided to return believing that there would be no reprisals against those who had served in the Obote government. He was driving in his car when another car approached and forced him to stop. He was never seen again.

A district commissioner and a hotel manager were arrested after a dispute with army officers over the payment of a hotel bill for drinks. They both disappeared. Three employees of the Coffee Marketing Board disappeared. A prominent Asian lawyer was arrested by two men identified as members of the State Research Department. Another Coffee Marketing Board worker vanished. These and other disappearances, arrests, and killings were carried out by the military police, the Public Safety Unit (a special police force), and the State Research Bureau (an intelligence unit).

In June 1972, a month before we arrived, George Kamba, a former ambassador to India and West Germany who served in the Amin government as director of the East African Posts and Telecommunications Corporation, was arrested while attending an official cocktail party at the International Hotel in Kampala. A witness told that Kamba, after leaving the hotel at about 10 P.M., came running back screaming for help. Three men with dark glasses followed him in and dragged him off. Kamba pleaded for help, shouting that they were going to kill him. Many leading personalities, including ministers, witnessed the seizure, but none could help. The men were armed and were believed to be part of Amin's State Research Bureau.

The official reaction of the government to these murders followed a pattern. First the government acknowledged the disappearance and ordered an investigation. The investigations usually revealed nothing, concluding that the people involved were missing and their whereabouts were unknown. In the case of Kamba's arrest, the official statement indicated that he was arrested by "unknown persons" and that extensive investigations had revealed nothing. Many people, unfortunately, believed these government explanations.

One of our briefings in Washington before we left for Kampala concerned and described the existence of bands of armed robbers in Uganda who often had no regard for life. Thievery exists in many societies; but in some, it is more open and prevalent. We in the United States, especially in the cities, have been plagued with the rise of muggings, rape, and other violent crimes. When I served on the U.S. Mission to the United Nations in New York in the fall of 1970 at the twenty-fifth anniversary session of the United Nations, I often had to warn visiting delegations to beware of walking in the parks and along streets alone at night.

In Uganda, roving bands of robbers were called *kondos*. Many Ugandans and foreigners had been victims of their attacks. The Uganda government under Milton Obote had tried to crack down on these criminals. In 1968, the punishment for robbery with violence was raised to that of a capital offense. With this severe punishment, Ugandan officials hoped to frighten *kondos* into refraining from violence. Some claimed that the severity of the law encouraged hardened criminals to be even more violent since they would be more likely to kill any witnesses to a robbery.

The existence of bands of criminals in Uganda made the atmosphere ripe for the soldiers to carry on their arbitrary arrests and killings under the guise of *kondoism*. The government issued two decrees in March 1971 that gave the military wide powers in searching and arresting. The decrees were described as a method of stemming the rampant *kondoism*. In effect, it legalized the killer squads of Amin, and also transformed some soldiers into *kondos*. Realizing that they had become the law, many soldiers found this an easy way to amass a small fortune. The police were rendered ineffective. Therefore, the soldier would not be held accountable for his actions. He was, in essence, the instrument of the law. He possessed weapons and could easily demand from the citizenry what he wished. Cars, watches, jewelry, money, and even wives were soon considered fair booty for the marauding soldiers.

A favorite item to steal was automobiles. Going down a lonely road, especially at night, one risked meeting a group of *kondos* who forced the driver to stop and give up the car. After several months, *kondoism* by Amin's squads became even more prevalent. Cars would be stopped in broad daylight, often by another car carrying three or four armed men. Most diplomats gave the advice to their fellow countrymen to give up the car without a struggle rather than risk one's life. The automobiles that were stolen were hardly ever retrieved. As the law and order of the country deteriorated, police did not dare lift a finger to find the suspects, for they never knew if the evidence that they would uncover would implicate the military. If their investigation did lead to the military, it was as good as committing suicide. The police officers involved would quickly be listed as having disappeared. Those making complaints to police regarding stolen automobiles often were advised to forget about retrieving the car and claim the insurance.

There are indeed other societies in which the military have assumed police power. In some, there has been sufficient military discipline to stem the temptation of the military to brutalize the citizenry for the sake of personal gain. In the case of Uganda, military discipline had already begun the process of deterioration as early as independence. Amin himself had avoided being court-martialed at least twice. Discipline to him meant mere loyalty to one's commander, and little else.

Amin shrewdly veiled his killings by soldiers and masked the elimination of certain civilians and military officers under the guise of *kondoism*. The people were fooled, for it was easy to confuse civilian-dressed soldiers with bands of *kondos*.

Amin, however, was not able to continue this charade. The people finally realized that certain branches of the military had been charged with killing their own countrymen. In September and October of 1972, large-scale disappearances took place. The government continued to give the same insufficient answers, and by then the people comprehended the full horror of Amin's regime.

On September 17, 1972, about one thousand supporters of Obote crossed the frontier in an effort to invade Uganda. They managed to enter Uganda easily; but as they moved north, they were quickly repelled by Ugandan forces. Amin was furious. He ordered his planes to drop bombs on the neighboring Tanzanian towns, and he unleashed his wrath on countless numbers of Ugandans whom he suspected to be potential enemies of his regime.

We have analyzed Amin's statements, as well as testimonies of various Ugandan government officials who have defected. We have read the reports of the International Commission of Jurists and other groups who have submitted material to the United Nations Commission on Human Rights. Finally, we have listened to the stories of many Ugandans now in exile. We believe that the names of those who disappeared in the latter part of 1972 were already listed for elimination before September of the same year.

The pattern regarding the murders of prominent people is so similar that it could only be executed according to plan. Amin had made critical statements regarding a number of officials or former officials. He therefore had decided already to eliminate them. The invasion of the forces from Tanzania only provided an excuse for his ruthless attack on several segments of the Ugandan society.

Much of the attack at the end of 1972 was centered on intellectuals. Amin feared them because they could easily see through his brutal actions. He knew that they mocked his unschooled manners and crude methods. Most of all, he felt threatened by them.

His other threat came from government officials. They were next.

On August 21, 1972, the daily newspaper, the *Uganda Argus*, reported that Amin had attacked high officials in the Masaka district—a stronghold of the Baganda tribe. He particularly singled out one who held a very high position in government who was dividing the country on a religious basis and claimed that the government had already lost confidence in him as a result of his "dirty activities."

There was no doubt that he was referring to Benedicto Kiwanuka, who was then serving as chief justice of Uganda's High Court. Kiwanuka, the country's first prime minister, had been a staunch Muganda Catholic. He had been imprisoned by Obote and released by Amin. After that he had made some very courageous decisions that went against the government, declaring that the military had no power to arrest. At a cocktail party, Kiwanuka remarked, "I am expecting them to come and take me soon. There is nothing to do but wait."

About the same time, we had received the warning about Joe Mubiru and other Baganda friends of ours and had passed the warning on to Joe.

As Uganda troops were mopping up the remnants of the invasion force of Obote supporters from Tanzania in September 1972, armed soldiers burst into the High Court chambers and took Kiwanuka, whom they handcuffed and slapped. He was taken away in a waiting car. Many people in the court and outside were witnesses to the arrest but the government's official statement claimed that the men who had kidnapped the chief justice had posed as security men. They claimed no knowledge of the affair. In the meantime, Wanume Kibedi, a brother-in-law of Amin who was serving as foreign minister, heard of Kiwanuka's arrest from Amin himself. On the very morning of the arrest, Kibedi claims that Amin said to him, "The boys have got Kiwanuka. They had to pick him up at the High Court because he knew he was being followed, and he was very careful about his movements."

The International Commission of Jurists have published that Kiwanuka was later seen by a witness in Makindye Prison. It was reported that he was killed with a sledgehammer. Another report claims an even more gruesome death for the chief justice which David Martin, a British journalist, quotes in his book, *General Amin*, "I was given to understand that his ears, nose, lips, and arms were cut and severed from his body. I also understand that he was disemboweled and his private parts cut and pushed into his mouth and he was finally burnt." Another witness claims that he took two hours to die.

The official government statement said, "So far, no evidence has come to light as to who arrested the chief justice and where he is.''

I had first met the chief justice when, in the early 1960s, he was visiting Catholic universities in the U.S., arranging scholarships for Ugandan students. Kiwanuka was the guest at a reception given by Catholic leaders in New York. He had called on Cardinal Spellman, who was helpful in obtaining scholarships for Ugandan students.

All who met him were impressed by his commitment to build the structures of a just society in Uganda. Our meeting was during a high point of idealism in New York. We were never able to call on him in Uganda, and within a few months after our arrival in 1972, he was brutally murdered.

We have no doubt that Amin was directly responsible for this notorious murder of the chief justice of Uganda.

Another victim, first smeared as an Obote spy, and then eliminated, was Frank Kalimuzo, vice chancellor and virtual head of the University of Makerere. The university had been founded fifty years previously. With an excellent reputation, it had a distinguished faculty including many scholars from all over the world. Amin accused Kalimuzo of being a spy for the neighboring country of Rwanda, charging that he wished to replace the vice chancellor with a ''real Ugandan.'' In September 1972, he was arrested and then released. One day while Kalimuzo was attending a wedding, Radio Uganda announced that he had disappeared. Learning of this announcement, he refused to flee, and was arrested the following day at his home. On October 7, all diplomats were invited to be present at the University of Makerere's graduation ceremonies. Amin, in his role as chancellor, appeared in full academic robes. Kalimuzo was conspicuously absent, but not a word was said. The diplomatic corps took their seats reluctantly, for many felt that they were in the presence of a man responsible for the murder of the institution's respected leader.

The university has since been on the verge of collapse. Many of its professors who were foreign nationals left. Many of its Ugandan professors also fled. Students were harassed and killed. In fact, in 1976, the students of the university staged one of the

41

George M. Kamba, first Ugandan ambassador to Vatican, being received by Pope Paul VI in 1969. He was later killed by Amin's agents.

Uganda's Chief Justice Benedicto Kiwanuka, who was tortured and killed, by Amin's agents.

only public protests against the Amin regime. They were courageous and perhaps rash, and they suffered as a result.

Perhaps one of the most horrifying episodes during the host of disappearances that occurred in the wake of the September invasion was the killing of Francis Walugembe, the former mayor of Masaka. On September 22, the former mayor was taken by one of Amin's henchmen to the Tropic Inn in Masaka. They called for drinks and then the army officer began to verbally abuse Walugembe. The former mayor was taken outside and stripped naked. It was morning and there were witnesses around the small hotel, which is located on a major highway. The victim's hands and ankles were tied together, and as he stood in front of the arresting army officer, a soldier slashed off his penis and held it in front of his face. Walugembe screamed in agony and was thrown into the back of a vehicle.

This scene of horror took place in full public view in the town of Masaka, only a short distance from a school were Margaret had once planned to teach. We had visited Masaka and had eaten at the Tropic Inn on a recent visit to the school where Margaret had reminisced about the plans she had had more than ten years previously.

Masaka was a sleepy little market town on Lake Victoria. Situated in the heart of Buganda, it was the center for many of the large land owners whose farms produced an array of vegetables and other crops. Only eighty miles from Kampala, it was a pleasant day's trip which took the traveler across the equator at about 4,000 to 5,000 feet. The town also had a large Asian population, which, by September, had already been thinned by the order of expulsion. The horrible scene that took place at the end of September 1972, gripped the Baganda people in fear. The Baganda had suffered under Obote, and Amin, as army commander, had led the attack on their king's palace. At the time of the coup, Amin had sought the Baganda as allies, releasing many of the political prisoners including Kiwanuka, whom he named chief justice. Yet, a year and a half later, Amin turned on the Baganda, criticizing and threatening their leaders. The plans laid by the invading force from Tanzania had set two geographic goals—Masaka and Mbarara. Amin used the threat of this invading force to carry out his plans against the Baganda—Kiwanuka, Walugembe, our friend Joe Mubiru, and many others became victims of Amin's bloodthirsty rule.

Part of the troops of the invading force crossed over the Tanzanian border and headed toward the army camp at Mbarara, which they almost succeeded in penetrating. After the abortive attempt, Amin was furious with the people of the region of Mbarara, some of whom were said to have cheered the insurgents. Many in the Ankole district where Mbarara is located were arrested and killed. Basil Bataringaya was dismembered alive and his head was displayed in the Mbarara barracks at the end of a pole for all to see the savagery of Amin's henchmen.

In Kampala, the diplomatic corps heard with dismay about the numerous disappearances. Within Uganda, the people were informed constantly that various persons were missing and that the government was unable to trace their whereabouts. However, the people whispered of the deaths and the cruel methods of killing. Large numbers fled Uganda in fear across the borders to Kenya and Tanzania.

About twenty countries maintained and housed diplomatic missions in Kampala. Diplomats from these missions were constantly barraged by exaggerated tales, and while in Kampala, one could not be sure of the accuracy of these accounts. These stories were not fully accepted until refugees from Uganda independently gave the same basic accounts.

Fear erupted almost spontaneously one day in September 1972. Word had passed through the streets of Kampala of some impending danger. In a moment, Ugandans were rushing through the streets in a panic to reach the safety of their homes. At our residence high on top of one of Kampala's seven hills, we could see African men and women running from places of work down the hillside toward the center of town. Cars raced on the roads. Instantly, news of this panic reached outside of Uganda; and in almost a flash, the telephone rang in my office. It was Assistant Secretary of State David Newsom calling from the State Department in Washington to inquire about what was happening. No one was sure. Immediately the embassy began calling families. Margaret was warned of the panic at our residence, where a number of children were swimming. She proceeded to gather the children into the house and to telephone all their mothers. We waited; still nothing was happening—no gunfire, no apparent attack, no news from the radio, only the spread of fear throughout the Ugandan population of Kampala. Within a few hours, everything was calm. The people had been so tense that a mere rumor was able to cause panic.

The next month a meeting was called at our residence for all Peace Corps volunteers to discuss the dangerous security situation in Uganda and the evacuation of Peace Corps members.

During the meeting, Margaret was called down to the front door, located on the ground floor of our residence. Standing in the hallway was a Ugandan man, trembling with fear. He was dressed in pajamas, with unkempt hair, and scratches on his arms and face. In between breaths and swallows, he managed to tell Margaret his name and where he had worked. He kept asking to see me and insisting that he was seeking asylum. The man was practically hysterical with fright. Margaret moved him upstairs to a private room where she was able to piece his story together. He had worked in a Ugandan government office where I had recently met him. The night before, soldiers had come to his home looking for him. Luckily, he was able to slip out of his house and climb a tree. He stayed in the tree all night waiting for a safe moment to come down. He did not return to his house but continued to hide, until he finally came to our residence. We did not know if he had been followed and we had to assume that someone working at our residence was being paid to inform the Ugandan government of the comings and goings at our home. I slipped out of the meeting long enough to convince our Ugandan friend to leave our residence in the company of an embassy officer. Contact was made with some of his friends and he managed to cross the border into Kenya.

The experience had brought us even closer to the anguish and terror of living in a country where one's life was held precariously in the hands of a cruel tyrant and his undisciplined soldiers.

The fear that gripped the nation—the terror, the bloodthirsty killings, and the obvious planned elimination—made us believe that Amin's regime was approaching a tyranny similar to that of

45

the Nazi leader, Hitler. There are so many comparisons to be made between the Amin regime and Nazi rule—the cruel tortures, the killer squads, the anti-intellectualism, the reprisals, the aggressive war posture, and above all, racism. By October, Amin's expulsion order against Asians was already well on the way to being carried out. Amin's attitude against the Israelis had developed into open anti-Semitic statements, and furthermore, an embrace of Hitler and his actions.

Diplomats, including ourselves, were beginning to see the full implications of Amin's statements and actions. We were reluctant to believe the almost incredible—that someone would actually declare his admiration for Hitler. We would have liked to pass over it as a sadistic joke or excuse Amin by declaring his inability to comprehend what he had said. But we were gradually realizing that Amin was, in many ways, a man of his words. One could never believe his exaggerated and boasting remarks, nor his cover-up attempts. One could never believe his promises for safety or fairness. But one could always take his threats seriously.

The evolution of an authoritarian dictatorship in Uganda into a cruel, bloodthirsty, and racist tyranny escaped the full evaluation of many in the diplomatic and foreign communities in Kampala. There were too many other events to contend with. First, the diplomats had their own nationals to worry about. The British had to deal with the monumental task of resettling scores of Asians. Other embassies as well were drawn into the Asian question by facilitating the immigration into their own countries of large numbers of Asians considered to be stateless.

The invasion of Uganda by Obote supporters in September 1972 had also created some difficult situations for a number of foreign nationals. The police and army rounded up many foreigners considered to be suspicious. First on this list were newsmen. One American journalist, Andrew Torchia of the Associated Press, was taken with a group of other reporters to the dreaded Makindye Military Prison. Fearing that he would have the same fate as Stroh and Siedle, I had immediately set to work on pressuring the Uganda government for information. We prayed that he was still alive. Finally, I obtained his release. It was a moment of great relief for me to see Andrew Torchia safely on the plane for London.

After he left Uganda, Torchia filed an Associated Press story of his arrest. While in Makindye, he saw merciless beatings during which others stood around and laughed, enjoying the spectacle.

In the meantime, Louis Morton, of Houston, Texas, a Peace Corps trainee, was killed on the road near Mbarara, where fighting had broken out between Ugandan units and the invaders. Morton was leaving the Peace Corps after the training period and had decided to visit the Queen Elizabeth game park before his departure. He and another trainee, Robert Freed, of Madison, Wisconsin, were driving back in a rented Volkswagen. Not knowing about the invasion, they proceeded to return to Kampala. They had been stopped and allowed to pass at two points on the road, but still they had no awareness of the danger. They then approached another roadblock. This time the soldiers opened fire. Morton was apparently killed instantly and Freed escaped into the brush.

We were saddened by the death of Louis Morton. I was particularly concerned, for his death was senseless. There would not have been a murder if certain regulations on traveling had been followed. On the other hand, the fear that permeated Uganda hardly encouraged the following of regulations.

Too many people refuse the advice of their embassy or state department. They take foolish and unnecessary chances with their lives. Many Americans, especially tourists who have little knowledge about the culture of the country to which they travel, believe that they can conduct themselves in the same manner as they do in the United States. What many do not realize is that there are few countries outside of their own where individual rights are held in high esteem.

In Uganda, the law is the gun held in the hands of a soldier— often undisciplined, illiterate, and sometimes drunk. Diplomats are supposed to be accorded special privileges. They cannot be arrested or searched. These fine points of international law are not known or understood by some governmental officials who have not been thoroughly trained. At a previous post, Margaret had been stopped by a guard for inadvertently driving her car into an exit instead of an entrance. The guard wanted to take her to the police station. She observed first that he was unarmed, so she tried to explain her diplomatic status. He did not understand and became insistent. Finally, a friend of the guard passed by and overheard the discussion. He assured his friend that Margaret was correct and the guard let her go. In Uganda, Margaret was not permitted to drive her own car. We employed a chauffeur to insure that she would not be held responsible for any accident or even minor infraction. There was no point in taking any chances.

Roadblocks were especially dangerous. Again, the diplomatic license and the ambassadorial flag on the car should have immediately conveyed to the soldiers or policemen that we were diplomats and should not be searched. If soldiers were manning the barriers, we would sometimes be told to get out of the car, and the contents of our car would be searched. Even the presentation of our passports or identification cards would not produce a reaction on the part of the searching soldiers. A few, not knowing how to read, would observe our papers upside down, until a nearby policeman, whose training was usually more advanced than the soldiers, would come to our rescue explaining that we were diplomats.

In sensitive areas—airports, military installations, and presidential offices—guards frequently carry machine guns. One evening all the ambassadors were called to be present at the State House in Entebbe—the official residence of the President. As each car approached the gate, a team of soldiers would approach from both sides, stick a machine gun in the window of the car, look around, observe one's identification, and then satisfied, would withdraw and wave the car forward. One slip on the machine gun and a crowd of people could be cut in two. We knew that, and thus we were always patient and calm when questioned, trying to avoid any quick gesture which could be misunderstood.

It was sometimes frustrating to try to convey the same concern for security to other Americans. Embassy officials would warn Americans about crossing borders by car: Soldiers at these crossings were often isolated from their companies and found that they could profit by demanding a price for permission to cross. Yet many persisted in ignoring this advice. Traveling into remote areas was discouraged by embassy personnel. Missionaries who were familiar with the country, language, and people, and who were prepared to accept whatever might occur were expected to ignore this advice. But others, seeing no external signs of danger, often believed that embassy people were by nature jittery. A missionary traveling along the road during the September invasion would probably have picked up quickly, from the roadblocks and the people along the way, the feeling that something unusual and dangerous was occurring. The two young American Peace Corps trainees, unfortunately, did not assess the situation accurately.

After the September invasion, the State Department was warning that travel to Uganda might be dangerous. Margaret's parents had planned to visit us. They were excited about their first trip abroad, and thus equally disappointed when they were told that it would be unsafe. For a few moments, Margaret considered phoning them from Kampala to tell them to disregard that advice, but this was a very selfish reaction. One or two more Americans in Uganda—relatives or not—would only mean a few more lives to worry about. It was unpredictable and, therefore, unsafe. Her parents never came.

On the same weekend of the September invasion, an American television personality, Joan Murray, arrived in Uganda as part of a U.S. Information Agency tour. She was staying at the hotel in the center of Kampala. After the invasion, the soldiers went through the hotel arresting all the foreign reporters. (Torchia had been taken while eating dinner.) I drove to the hotel and suggested to Joan Murray that she stay at our residence for the remainder of her visit; we did not want her to risk being arrested. We had gone to the Central Police Station in Kampala and had found several Peace Corps members, missionaries, and two tourists. They and other foreign nationals were being held in one common room in the basement of the police station. There was a European family there with a small child. They were dirty and tired, and the child was irritable after being confined for so long. The room smelled of sweat and urine. After finding them, we brought food to them regularly until we could arrange for their release. We fortunately found rank to be an asset in this case. Others of lesser diplomatic rank sometimes would have difficulty in seeing the prisoners, but at the slightest hesitance, I would loudly insist that as ambassador I had a right to see the imprisoned nationals. In the damp cellar of the police station there were other cells in which Africans were held. Although we did not know it at the time, one of our friends from student days in New York was there. He had been picked up about the same time as Joe Mubiru, but luckily he was arrested by the police and not by Amin's killer squad. Margaret learned of his imprisonment when she met his wife in the local supermarket. The setting proved to be an excellent place to gather information. In the days that followed, Margaret was able to remain in contact with Ugandan women friends by meetings in that supermarket.

We remember when we first came into contact with the African students in New York how amazed we were at the methods of communication used between student groups. We of the West would think in terms of sending reams of written communications to invoke a meeting or propagandize a point of view. Our African friends used word of mouth. Without spending any money on mimeographed notices, they were able to convoke meetings of students and friends from diverse parts of the country in a relatively short amount of time with seemingly little effort.

While we were in Uganda, we developed a sense of this African way of communication. Underneath, the people began to realize exactly what was happening. There was a pervading sense of fear.

As Ugandans were being arrested and killed, many diplomats were preoccupied with the troubles of their own citizens. The Asian expulsion, the invasion and its aftermath, commanded the attention of the international community. The eyes of the world were diverted from the vicious extermination policy being carried out by Amin and the special agencies he had designated as responsible for committing the brutal murders.

But it was to be only the beginning.

4: AMIN: VICIOUS ANTI-SEMITE

THE FIRST RECORDED WORDS OF IDI AMIN AFTER HE SEIZED power in January 1971, were, "I am not a politician, but a professional soldier. I am, therefore, a man of few words. . . ."

Despite Amin's lack of formal education, he is shrewd in his dealings with the international community. He has an uncanny sense of the dramatic and his timing is superb. While he has said that he is a man of few words, he delights in being quoted in the news media. It was a great boost to his ego to have the French make a film about him. He was the star in the film, and evidently had been quite pleased with his performance until he read the reviews which mocked and criticized him.

He is a master at creating international headlines. He has learned to use this skill not only as a public-relations gimmick, but to divert world attention from the massive killings taking place in Uganda.

Even during my first meeting with Idi Amin, I had listened to Amin complain almost theatrically about U.S. involvement in Vietnam and other matters. In the same interview, Amin had warned about Israelis coming to Uganda on U.S. passports. He also warned that tourists should not wander into remote areas of the country, for "some bad people might harm them." In August, two incidents involving Americans verified the insecure conditions of traveling in Uganda. A U.S. diplomat and his wife, on their way back to Rwanda, were stopped at the Ugandan border. The soldiers threatened the American woman but were finally talked out of harming her. Another group of tourists were roughed up by soldiers at the game park near the Zaïre border. One woman was slapped by a soldier. The tourists involved had obvious Jewish names.

We were both still plagued by Amin's anti-Israeli posture and his apparent suspicion that any Jew could be an Israeli agent working to destroy him. Then, on September 12, 1972, Amin made such an extraordinary statement that it was difficult to believe. However, by this time diplomats had learned that Amin's announcements were not to be taken lightly. He had already begun a full-scale expulsion of Asians, including Ugandan citizens. This time his announcement took the form of cabled messages to Secretary General Waldheim at the United Nations and Premier Golda Meir of Israel. In these telegrams Amin said, "Germany is the place where when Hitler was the Prime Minister and Supreme Commander, he burned over six million Jews. This is because Hitler and all German people knew that Israelis are not people who are working in the interest of the world and that is why they burned the Israelis alive with gas in the soil of Germany." Furthermore, Amin criticized those countries which had condemned the terrorist killings of Israeli athletes at the Olympic games in Munich and charged that Israel should be condemned and removed from the United Nations.

Besides his shocking approval of Hitler's killing of the Jews, Amin also called for the removal of Israelis to Britain. Amin himself had viewed the Asian presence in East Africa as a fault of the British. To rid Uganda of these brown-skinned people, he expelled them and sent most of them to Britain. Having been told of Britain's role in establishing the State of Israel, he now offered a similar solution to the problem of the Middle East. "Palestine is for the Palestinians," he said, "and not for the Israelis who had been taken there by Britain, the crooks who have made mistakes everywhere in the world in marking the boundaries of the countries they formerly occupied as colonizers."

Amin's statement in support of Hitler convinced us that Amin was a confirmed anti-Semite. The official U.S. State Department reaction called Amin's description of the holocaust "deeply shocking and incomprehensible in any context but particularly when it comes from a national leader."

Amin's approval of the holocaust was an obscene insult to human justice. I was instructed by the Department of State to raise objections to Amin's telegrams at the most effective level. I immediately requested a meeting with Amin. The United States was the only government to protest directly to Amin on the matter. It is a credit to our government that when others were silent, we at least raised our voice.

The meeting with Amin took place at his command post. This consisted of a comfortable house in a residential area of Kampala surrounded by lush gardens and soldiers carrying machine guns. Amin was more subdued than I expected. He sat in a modestly furnished room. His huge frame, which had grown portly, filled his comfortable armchair almost entirely. After I had delivered our government's message, Amin made no real attempt to change his approval of Hitler's genocide against the Jewish people.

Normally, the press coverage of a diplomat's meeting contains long descriptions of what was said by Amin. The announcement this time from President Amin's office was relatively short. It claimed that he had said he was misinterpreted and that he was not against Jews but against Zionists.

I was convinced that Amin's anti-Semitic statements were so severe that Jews were not safe in Uganda. Within a few days of the meeting, I ordered the immediate evacuation of Jews on the embassy staff, and strongly urged that Jewish members of technical assistance programs and private American groups leave also.

Not only were Amin's statements alarming, but the security in Uganda for foreigners had deteriorated rapidly. The departing Asians were being molested and robbed. Tourists were being stopped and threatened. Two American youths were arrested and held briefly because their long hair made soldiers suspicious. Tension had increased. Amin also announced that all visitors were to enter and leave the country at the airport and through the main rail and road links to Kenya. He warned of foreigners entering Uganda under "suspicious" circumstances.

Margaret held a meeting for the wives of U.S. diplomats and aid personnel. Normally, the ambassador's wife looks forward to this first meeting of American women, hoping to learn about women's projects and interests and looking forward to cooperating on future projects. But at this meeting, Margaret had to speak quite bluntly to the wives present. She noted that it would probably be difficult for many who had been involved in projects with Ugandan women and children to continue. All foreigners were suspect. She had learned from some Ugandan women that it was dangerous for them to have American volunteers working directly with them. Margaret also warned them that the situation in Uganda was already unsafe and would probably become worse instead of better for Americans and their families. It was a gloomy moment for her, for she would much rather have been optimistic and positive at this first meeting. She had for a long time been a volunteer in the field of relations between American and African women and would have liked to urge the women present to increase their own activities and propose new projects. This was impossible. Instead, she urged them to take security precautions and to look for ways to keep up the morale of their families and friends during these difficult times.

Finally I called in the American-Jewish members of my staff and announced the decision to evacuate. Next, I met personally with every one of the Jewish members of technical assistance programs. Some were doctors working on cancer and other research programs in conjunction with the hospital and university in Kampala. Most saw the logic of my reasoning. They and their families were in danger because they were Jews. It was a horrid fact that after the misery of the Nazi holocaust, their Jewishness made them once again targets of extreme racism. A few objected to my arguments, for they did not practice their religion nor did they exercise any form of Zionism. All but one couple left within a few weeks. Each time a Jewish staff member or private American left, we felt relieved, as we were convinced that there was a clear and present danger to their lives.

The next week I received a telephone call from a newsman in Nairobi. He asked if it were true that Jews were being evacuated from Kampala. Knowing that the phones were probably tapped, I deliberately denied it. I did not want a public announcement to take place while Jews were still in the country, because I feared that Amin might become enraged, and in retaliation, threaten the lives of the remaining Jews. Amin would simply label one of the Jewish Americans as a Zionist or Israeli agent and have the person condemned to death, or he might arrange to have the person disappear or killed in a car accident.

A week after the evacuation of the Jewish Americans, the September invasion of Uganda by Obote forces from Tanzania took place during which the Peace Corps trainee Louis Morton was killed. The embassy team believed that the deteriorating situation warranted taking steps to drastically reduce the number of Americans in Uganda.

As with the evacuation of Jewish members, the departure of the Peace Corps needed to be carried out as quietly and as quickly as possible. Therefore, a withdrawal was designed and orchestrated and quietly carried out.

Our embassy staff cooperated and put in many long hours in accomplishing the difficult task of bringing Peace Corps men and women to Kampala and then arranging for their departure. Not every Peace Corps member agreed with the decision to withdraw. Deeply involved and committed to various grass-roots projects, some felt that we were doing the Ugandan people a disservice by leaving.

Not everyone agreed that the withdrawal should be done without announcing it. In fact, some correspondents accused the State Department of "cowering before a little tyrant." They urged the U.S. to take more positive steps in showing our disapproval of Amin's words and actions. They suggested that the U.S. government end all technical assistance and announce the stoppage of all loans. There was one flaw in these arguments. We were not dealing with an ordinary dictator—but with a brutal murderer.

In effect, our Peace Corps program and our other technical assistance programs were being phased out—but gradually and in steps. The first objective was to evacuate as many Americans as possible, for their lives were worth more than a few slaps at Amin. I felt that no chances should be taken when it came to innocent lives.

The evacuation was completed by November. Every Peace Corps member had safely left Uganda. In addition, many of the dependents of our AID mission had gone. Families who went home did not return. Personnel who completed their assignments were not replaced. When we arrived in Uganda, the number of Americans was estimated to be around one thousand. By November, that number was cut in half.

One aspect of the Peace Corps evacuation that disturbed me was that I could not be totally candid with the press. I received several phone inquiries from reporters in Nairobi. In addition to realizing that our telephone conversations were probably monitored, I did not want to risk thrusting the matter into the headlines. I knew Amin was very sensitive to news coverage. He enjoyed being the star in the news media—as long as he was the winner. But if he were the loser—he often would angrily retaliate in order to teach his "opponent" a lesson. Amin could easily have arranged for a Peace Corps member to be assaulted, or disappear on the way from Kampala to Entebbe airport.

To avoid giving information to the press when they specifically request it is not easy. I still firmly believe that during both the Jewish and Peace Corps evacuations, tempting Amin's anger could have endangered the lives of innocent persons. That was 1972. Obviously, subsequent events have demonstrated Amin's total disregard for human life.

One can't help but wonder if Idi Amin, the tyrant of Uganda, would have half as much press coverage if he did not expound on extraordinary subjects or create the ugly incidents that he does. The fact that he was responsible for the killing of 100,000 Ugandans may not have been quite as newsworthy as his support of the guerrilla hijacking of an Air France plane. We shudder to think that the Western press may have been more interested in Amin's threats to the British, Americans, and Israelis than in the extermination of certain Ugandan people. In a sense, the fact that there has been coverage of these international incidents has also brought to the attention of the world the many reports from witnesses to Amin's brutal acts against his own people.

On the other hand, the international incidents caused by Amin have diverted the attention of the U.S. and other foreign governments from the horrid acts he has committed against his own people. It actually seems that when he senses that a foreign government is about to criticize him or cut back in aid, Amin throws them off balance by devising some threat or complication as a warning. While the foreign government mobilizes its foreign office to deal with the current problem, Amin uses the moment to eliminate a few more people.

Amin delights in seeing people squirm. There are stories of how people marked for death are brought before him pleading for mercy. In a devil-like fashion, he ridicules them and sends them to be killed. Likewise, he particularly enjoys having major powers cower before him. His favorite pastime is humiliating his former colonial masters, the British.

To create international incidents and to needle the British and others in the Western world, he has used minority groups as scapegoats in his attacks. During our stay in Uganda, Amin turned his wrath on two groups—the Jews and the Asians. In both tragic episodes, Amin showed his perverted view of justice and his fanatical racist mind.

The first of the scapegoats were the Israelis. Israel had come to Amin's aid after his coup in 1971. In less than a year and a half, Amin was finished with the Israelis. After kicking them out, he turned on them viciously. His alignment with the Arab states shifted to an espousal of the most radical of the Palestinian causes. His attack on the Israelis sank into a fierce hatred of Jews.

Amin had first come into contact with the Israelis during the early period of Ugandan independence. The Israelis were aiding the southern Sudanese rebels who were fighting Arab domination from the north. Amin, being from the West Nile region of Uganda on the southern Sudanese border, was also interested in cementing relationships between the southern Sudanese and the Ugandans. Indeed many of the tribes of the West Nile area straddled the border between Sudan and Uganda.

Refugees from Uganda now speak of large numbers of Nubians and Anyanya from Sudan in the Ugandan army. Amin probably began recruiting these southern Sudanese before his coup d'état on several trips that he took with Israeli advisers. In 1969, Ugandan President Milton Obote launched an effort to bring about reconciliation between the southern Sudanese and the Arab-dominated Sudanese government. With the war likely to come to an end, the Anyanya guerrillas were more than happy to consider employment with Amin.

Many believe that Colonel Bar-Lev, the head of the Israeli military mission in Kampala, must have known something about Amin's plans for a coup. Whether or not this was true, Amin received Israeli support once he gained power. Israel was already involved with military training of the Ugandan army. Military equipment, including some captured Arab tanks from the Six Day War, had already been supplied to Uganda. Israeli military advisers, such as Colonel Bar-Lev, enjoyed familiarity and influence with Ugandan military officers. The Israelis had also trained some of the police and were providing training programs for the air force. Amin himself had gone to Israel in 1963 for a paratrooper course. He continues to wear the wings he received on that program.

The tide began to turn when Amin made a trip to Israel in July 1971. He assured the Israelis of Uganda's good relations and promised to open an embassy in Jerusalem. Then he asked the Israelis for more military and economic aid and talked of planning an invasion of Tanzania. The Israelis wanted no part of Amin's wild scheme but decided to give him a limited supply of armaments and an executive jet. Amin went to Britain to have lunch with the Queen and approach the British for jet fighter planes. They refused.

We heard people say that Amin was already tired of the Israelis. They had helped him into power by supporting the army and his alliance with the southern Sudanese; but he wanted to run his own show and their advisers sometimes interfered. He might have feared that they would eventually be able to overthrow him, for they knew his weaknesses.

In essence, it was hopeless for Amin to think that he would receive military equipment from Britain, the West, or from Israel to invade a neighboring African state. Perhaps he dreamed up the story so that he would be refused and, therefore, have an excuse to look for other allies.

As we reexamine Amin's words and actions, we become convinced that he is an imitator. He has a cunning and shrewd manner but cares nothing about the intricacies and delicacies of his actions. He was learning to be an African nationalist leader. Watching other African leaders, he wished to be welcomed into their company. He thus decided that he must develop an anticolonialist posture, but he did not think beyond that issue. He had no ideology or theories with which to replace the present Ugandan structure. He had overthrown Obote, who had recently turned toward socialism. He knew that he had to oppose Obote's policies and, thus, he disavowed socialism for Uganda. He could not be a socialist and he could not risk being directed by the Western "imperialists."

When the Israelis refused him, Amin had a brilliant idea. He could turn against the Israelis and become part of the Arab cause. This suited him very well. He remarked on his takeover of the Ugandan government that he was a professional soldier. He was, and is, still a soldier—but a soldier who thrives on war without any commitment to an ideal or cause. Joining the Arab forces immediately put Uganda into the state of war—if not physically, at least verbally.

In February 1972, Amin went to visit the Libyan president Muammar Qaddafi. Radio Uganda announced that Libya and Uganda had jointly pledged their support for "the struggle of the Arab people against Zionism and imperialism." It is significant that the end of the civil war in Sudan also came in February. No longer did the southern Sudanese need the aid of Israel. It provided a perfect moment for breaking away from Israel.

The Libyans dispatched a delegation to Kampala which promised economic aid to the country and assistance to the Moslem institutions. When the visit ended, Amin accused Israel of subversive activities and threatened to close the embassy. Despite this, Amin asked Israel for the deferment of payments on credits. On March 22, 1972, Amin announced that he would not renew any existing agreements between Uganda and Israel. He cancelled all armament orders from Israel and ordered work to stop on construction projects being handled by Israelis. He announced that Obote had become "almost a prisoner of Israel economically" and this was the source of Uganda's debt. He vowed not to make the same mistake. Finally, Amin ordered all Israelis to leave—and diplomatic relations were broken. On April 10, after all Israelis had been withdrawn from Uganda, Foreign Minister Abba Eban charged that Amin and Qaddafi of Libya had plotted to end Israel's presence in Uganda "in the most demonstrative and insulting way possible." He defended the assistance his country had given to Uganda over the decade and reminded the Ugandans that the value of equipment left in Uganda and payments due for labor and services amounted to between $15 and $20 million.

Amin blamed the deterioration of the Ugandan economy on the Israelis, when actually a good part of the difficulty lay in his heavy spending for military equipment and armaments. This had begun during the Obote period when Amin had been asked to account for the huge amount of money missing from the army budget. There was no doubt that Israel was the first of Amin's scapegoats.

In the wake of the Israeli departure, Amin began to accuse and insult the Israelis even more. He described his version of Israeli plans to sabotage Uganda's efforts and began to praise vociferously the Arab cause. He proposed plans to conquer Israel and offered his military assistance to the Arabs when they marched against it. He continually gave advice to all the Arab leaders, invited the Palestine Liberation Organization to come to Kampala, and even tried to install them in the Israeli embassy—until the Italian ambassador (the dean of the diplomatic corps) protested.

Practically every night we watched Amin's harangues before the television cameras, warning the people of imperialist and Zionist plots. At one point, he tried to convince the people that another invasion was imminent. He declared that destroyers were in the Indian Ocean and troops were crossing Lake Victoria. He convinced Colonel Qaddafi to send him military assistance, but the Sudanese government refused to allow Libya to fly its planes across the Sudan.

Following the elimination of so many prominent Ugandans in September and October 1972, there was little doubt that Amin was impersonating the man that he so admired—Adolf Hitler. But hardly any of my diplomatic colleagues wished to talk about "this man." So many of the diplomats represented countries that had suffered greatly from the brutality of Hitler; but no one wanted to say that Amin was a new Hitler.

There is a natural reluctance to recognize the reality of ongoing brutality. When I was recalled for consultations on October 22, I called on various European and African diplomatic colleagues. Some thought that Amin was only a fool. Others admitted the recent deaths, but felt that it would change for the better.

Surprisingly, I found a more realistic atmosphere in Washington, where there was general agreement that I should arrange for the rapid reduction of the official U.S. presence and encourage private Americans to leave.

After returning to Kampala on November 7, I again called on

many of my American and African colleagues. They remained generally reluctant to recognize the massive evidence that Amin was a brutal tyrant. Margaret and I both felt that the media had a better grasp of Amin's dangerous propensities than some of the professionals who were supposed to be experts in evaluating political leaders. There remained throughout 1972 a sentiment in Kampala diplomatic circles that somehow Amin would cease being a tyrant.

This never happened!

On November 15, we attended a state dinner in Kampala in honor of King Faisal of Saudi Arabia. The old king arrived in a flurry of pageantry to cement relations with Uganda and to deliver half of a promised loan. Amin alluded to the Saudi gift as being the answer to one of his many dreams. With the Asians gone and the Saudis acting as saviors, Amin promised the people that the economy was about to recover. All the diplomats in Kampala, heads of churches, and government ministries were present at the dinner. The small, stooped king sat modestly beside the huge, boasting figure of Amin. It did not surprise us that the king took the usual Arab position against Israel and Zionism. However, in the course of the dinner, a pamphlet was distributed—the *Protocols of the Elders of Zion*. We had heard about this violently anti-Jewish book, but this was the first time we had encountered it.

It was not until March, however, that the government controlled newspaper, the *Voice of Uganda*, reported that Amin intended to reproduce the document in all languages so that the people of Uganda and Africa might understand the dangers of Zionism. Amin was quoted as saying, "Israelis want to destroy God, and to be a Zionist, you must specialize in murder."

While we were in Uganda, we noticed a number of Palestinians settling in Kampala. With time, Amin became more and more allied with them and their numbers grew. Knowing the freedom with which they operated in Uganda, our own embassy became concerned with the possibility of a Palestinian terrorist operation within the Kampala diplomatic community. The terrorists struck—but it was in the Sudan region where they killed both the U.S. ambassador and his deputy.

The PLO entered into a more formal agreement with Amin in

March 1975. Palestinians were employed as Amin's personal bodyguards. A delegation was invited to join the meeting of the Organization of African Unity in July 1975. Finally, there was close military cooperation. In August, Radio Uganda quoted Amin as saying "Yasir Arafat had sent Palestinian pilots to join the Ugandan Air Force operations against imperialism in Africa." Using Russian MIG's, Ugandan pilots attempted to train Palestinians to fly the planes. A number of accidents were reported, and one Palestinian is known to have died in an air crash. At the beginning of 1976, Amin announced that he had allocated plots of land totaling several thousands of acres to the Palestinians. With an estimated four hundred Palestinians living near Entebbe, it was not surprising that the hijacked Air France plane headed to Uganda for sanctuary.

At the Organization of African Unity meeting in Kampala in July 1975, Amin became chairman of the African group. At that meeting, he joined extremists in demanding Israel's expulsion from the UN. In September, we assumed that Amin, in his role of OAU chairman, would come to New York to address the United Nations.

I wrote directly to President Ford on September 3, 1975, and urged him "to instruct the U.S. delegation to the UN General Assembly to be absent when Uganda's President Amin speaks to that body." In my letter, I went on to say:

> I urge you to take formal steps to indicate our disapproval of the actions of this tyrant because they are *gross violations of human rights* as distinguished from repression. I cite:
>
> 1. The established fact that he has since 1971 liquidated over 60,000 of his own people. Their murder normally follows hours of torture, which makes the death seem like a humane act. My enclosed article from *Worldview* will give you a few more of the details. This selective genocide is still going on. Almost every week brings me a message about a Ugandan who is missing or dead. Amin has turned these deaths into a joking matter.
>
> 2. After the sufferings of the Ugandan Africans, the next group to suffer has been the Ugandan Asians. I was there in 1972 when Amin expelled over 50,000 Asians and saw the daily brutality. He has indicated no regret for this massive violation of human rights.

3. Amin continues to praise Hitler for his genocide against the Jews. He has now announced that a park will be named in his honor. While it seems incredible, there never has been a word of apology from him about the statement he issued while I was there in 1972 approving Hitler's holocaust against the Jews. This was a public obscenity of the crudest type and is a humiliation to all peoples, especially our own Jewish citizens.

4. I remain very suspicious of Amin's account of the murder of the two Americans, Nicholas Stroh and Robert Siedle. While this occurred before my tour of duty in Uganda, I, as a result of subsequent chats with Ugandans, believe that the matter of involvement in the murder of these two Americans by the highest levels of the Amin government cannot be eliminated.

The withdrawal of a U.S. diplomatic mission from Uganda in 1973 was one manifestation of the U.S. government's displeasure at the gross violations of human rights taking place in that country. Since then, the situation has become worse. While there are unfortunately cases of repression going on in various countries, none of them, at this time, equal the horror of both the ongoing selective genocide that is going on in Uganda and the obscene fact that President Amin still approves of Hitler's genocide against the Jews.

A simple, dignified, nonviolent indication of the U.S. government's disapproval of these acts would be the total absence of the U.S. delegation from the General Assembly when this tyrant is speaking. The reasons for this action should be announced.

High officials, and former superiors, in the State Department did respond to my recommendation to President Ford. The final decision was that the then chief of the U.S. Mission to the UN, Daniel P. Moynihan, would be absent but that other members would be present.

Amin's October 1 address to the UN General Assembly turned out as we feared. It was a gross public obscenity. Not only did Amin call for the expulsion of Israel from the UN, but he urged "the extinction of Israel as a State." Furthermore, he called upon the American people to "rid their society of the Zionists." His ninety-minute speech was read in English by Uganda's chief UN delegate. Afterwards, Amin himself spoke for another ten minutes. He received two standing ovations from delegates on the assembly floor.

At a news conference the next day, Amin said that New York City was bankrupt because the money of the innocent American people was taken to arm Israel. "Zionists own actually even the United States of America. . . . Surely it has been in the papers. Don't tell me you don't know this."

It was repugnant for us to see how this madman, stained with the blood of thousands of his own innocent people, could be applauded in the halls of the United Nations.

Our own chief delegate, Daniel P. Moynihan, who was not present for Amin's speech, had the courage to label Amin as a "racist-murderer." His expelling of Asians from Uganda, his tirades against various tribal groups within his own country, and his admiration for Hitler had confirmed the fact that he was a racist and anti-Semite. As he stood bedecked in medals, including the British Victoria Cross, Amin couched his racism in the rhetoric of independence and anticolonialism. It was truly a day of mourning for the United Nations.

When some delegates voiced their disapproval of Moynihan's "flamboyant and insulting" remarks, Moynihan did not retract his statement. Nor did the White House, which announced that President Gerald Ford supported Daniel Moynihan's terms.

In the meantime, the government newspaper in Uganda accused Moynihan of "diplomatic insanity." The paper continued to say that "President Amin never seconded the extermination, but rather recommended a pure coexistence of nationals. . . . This would dissolve the Jewish State of Israel. . . ."

We had seen many similar attempts by Ugandans serving in the civil service or in cabinet positions to explain Amin's extreme statements. His words often took by surprise his own officials, who constantly tried to excuse or reinterpret the meanings of his speeches. In all cases, it was no use. We learned while we were in Uganda that Amin meant every word he said despite the hemming and hawing of his ministers.

When he was at the United Nations, Amin declared that he personally liked Jews, but "I don't approve of Zionism." Many times he had said to one of his victims, "I like you very much.

You are my friend," and then ordered him killed. In April 1975, Radio Uganda reported that Amin praised the Germans—particularly Hitler—for their bravery, but he had been disappointed not to see Hitler's portrait or a monument to him in Berlin when he had traveled there. Furthermore, Amin was quoted that "although some people felt Adolf Hitler was bad, he was a great man and a real conquerer whose name would never be forgotten." He pledged to name a park and erect a monument in honor of Hitler.

Amin repeatedly reinforced his own statements on Hitler and his hatred for the Jewish people. Knowing this and his record of cruelty, no responsible person or country could possibly tolerate his speaking before the world body, let alone accord him any dignity of office.

Long after our return to the U.S., our worst fears finally came to life on our television screen as we watched reports of what had taken place in Uganda on the evening of June 29, 1976. In the old cement terminal building at Entebbe airport in Uganda, the names of eighty-three passengers of a hijacked Air France plane were read out by one of the Palestinian terrorists. These passengers were asked to move with their belongings into another room in the airport lounge. All the names were Jewish.

We watched and listened to the developments from our home in Philadelphia. We were horrified, for we knew Amin and how dangerous he could be. We knew well his support of the Palestinians. We knew well his admiration for Hitler and his approval of the Nazi extermination of six million Jews. The scene was so reminiscent of those terrifying years when Jews were hunted and singled out for the Nazi gas chambers. Now Amin had been given his chance to become a Hitler. Together with the Palestinians, to whom he had given sanctuary and assistance, Amin could relive in the eyes of the world the same sinister experiences of the Jewish holocaust.

Amin made frequent visits to the hijacked passengers that week in Entebbe. He claimed that he was negotiating for their release but constantly blamed the Israeli government for being obstinate in refusing to surrender to the Palestinian demands. He termed the demands generous and urged Israel to give in.

When the Air France plane had landed at Entebbe Sunday

Mrs. Dora Bloch, 75, was murdered by Amin's secret police after the successful Israeli raid on Entebbe.

morning, June 27, Amin met and embraced the hijackers, calling them freedom fighters. Other Palestinians living in Uganda came to Entebbe airport to help guard those on the plane. As the week passed, passengers observed the Palestinians arriving and leaving the airport in diplomatic cars. Ugandan soldiers relieved the Palestinian guards and supplied the terrorists with weapons. At one point, Ugandan soldiers joined in the questioning of Nachum Dahan, an Israeli with a French passport. Suspecting that he might be a member of the Israeli army, the terrorists slapped, punched, and twisted the fingers of Dahan, forcing him to write reports about Israel. At one point, a Ugandan soldier tore up a report claiming that this was not what was wanted. "We want to know about the army. We want to know where the bases are."

When the passengers had been led off the airplane to the terminal in Entebbe, they had been startled to see their pathway lined by Ugandan soldiers with rifles pointed. There was no question that the Ugandan army was guarding the passengers—not the terrorists. To us it was clear that Amin was a partner in the hijacking.

Finally, the non-Israeli passengers were released with the exception of the French crew, who refused to leave. Among the remaining hostages was a survivor of a Nazi concentration camp. His arm bore a tattooed number as a living reminder of the holocaust that took the lives of his parents.

As we were celebrating our country's bicentennial on July 4, Israel had decided to use military action to free the hostages. They had gathered intelligence from many sources. The Israelis had built part of the Entebbe airport and they knew it well. There were Israeli military officers who knew Amin and had worked with him before and shortly after he had come into power. They were well prepared and they succeeded. The Israeli Ambassador Chaim Herzog later explained the Israeli government position at the United Nations, "Following the never-to-be-forgotten experience of the holocaust in Europe during the Second World War, an oath was taken—whether consciously or unconsciously —by every member of the Jewish people wherever he or she might have been, that never again would this happen."

The Israeli rescue operation at Entebbe airport was spectacular.

In ninety minutes Israeli commandoes had freed the hostages, killed, photographed, and fingerprinted the terrorists; and destroyed some of the Russian MIG planes at the airport. A number of Ugandan soldiers were also killed. Only four Israelis met their death, one commando and three hostages. Amin was stunned. It was a humiliating defeat for him.

Unfortunately one hostage was left behind. Dora Bloch, a seventy-three-year-old woman, who possessed dual nationalities —Israeli and British—had been taken to the hospital the Friday before the raid. She and her son had been among the hostages. On the morning of July 4, after the early morning raid, a British diplomat went to the hospital in Kampala to check her condition. She was sleeping but nurses said she was well enough to return to the Entebbe airport. No one at the hospital seemed to know about the Israeli strike. When the officer returned with food for Mrs. Bloch, he was not permitted to enter. Later, it was rumored that she was dragged from her hospital room and thrown into an army vehicle. She was never seen again. When questioned about Mrs. Bloch's whereabouts, Amin said that she had been taken back to Entebbe before the raid. The British termed Amin's statement "rubbish," for an official had seen her after the rescue operation. Then the Ugandan authorities said that they knew nothing of her whereabouts and ceased to be responsible for the hostages after the Israeli raid. Less than a year later, Henry Kyemba, the minister of health in Uganda, defected and gave testimony regarding the death of Mrs. Bloch. He confirmed that she had been dragged from her hospital room by agents of the State Research Bureau. She shrieked and struggled, bringing hospital attendants and patients to their doors, but no one dared to lift a finger to save her. Still screaming, she was taken through the emergency room, but still no one answered her cries for help. Everyone was terrified. Mrs. Bloch was taken into the back seat of a waiting car. That was the last time she was seen alive.

Kyemba claimed that she "had been murdered to satisfy the President's lust for vengeance." When Kyemba met the President shortly after Mrs. Bloch had vanished, Amin said to him, "Oh, by the way, you know that woman? Forget her. They have already finished her."

Mrs. Bloch disappeared as did hundreds of others in Uganda. The government will not acknowledge her death. What would have happened to the hostages if they had not been rescued? Knowing Amin's record, we feared for their lives. Years later Amin's words of despicable racial hatred and anti-Semitism still ring in our ears from our Uganda stay.

In our early 1972 contacts with Amin, we did not want to believe that he endorsed the worst of Hitler's genocide; that he was anti-Semitic. We perhaps were not alone in that reluctance. Later, when we became convinced of his deep-rooted anti-Semitism, we recognized the disturbing similarity between the response of many people to Amin and the response of many Europeans and Americans to the clear anti-Semitism that came forth from Hitler in the early days of his rule in Germany.

The world must learn one simple lesson about brutal tyrants. At least the fact of their brutality and obsessions should be accepted. Denying the existence of brutality never changed it! The response of the world to Amin has been very similar to the pre-World War II response to Hitler.

5: THE EXPULSION OF THE ASIANS

JULY AND AUGUST ARE BEAUTIFUL MONTHS IN UGANDA—THE country that Winston Churchill described after his visit there in the early days of this century as the "pearl of Africa." The first two months of our assignment to Uganda were busy ones, getting acquainted and facing the ever increasing challenge of Idi Amin Dada.

We would, from time to time, steal a few minutes on a second-floor veranda at the residence and watch the sunset over Lake Victoria. The beauty of a peaceful sun setting could not erase our growing feeling that Idi Amin was more than a mercurial dictator. Equally depressing was our feeling that the flavor of such a once promising land was evaporating.

For despite being a land-locked country, astride the equator, Uganda has a great deal to offer its people. Most of the country lies between 3,000 and 6,000 feet above sea level, thus moderating the heat of the tropical sun. With huge Lake Victoria, almost half of which lies within Uganda's borders, and the numerous other lakes and tributaries that wind northward to form the Nile, most of the country possesses an adequate water supply. Uganda is comparatively small—about 91,000 square miles, or about the size of Oregon. Nevertheless, Winston Churchill admonished its British colonial developers, "Concentrate upon Uganda. Nowhere else will the results be more brilliant, more substantial, and more rapidly realized."

Before the coming of the Europeans, several centralized and well developed African kingdoms were present in the Great Lakes area of Eastern Africa. The Bunyoro kingdom on Lake Albert in western Uganda, and the Buganda kingdom on the northern shores of Lake Victoria were among these. By the nineteenth century, Buganda had increased its domain and consolidated its strength. The ruler of the kingdom of Buganda greeted the first British explorers who trekked inland from the East African coast in the 1860s in search of the source of the Nile.

The British extended their sphere of influence into Uganda through the Imperial British East Africa Company, a commercial

Map courtesy of University of Notre Dame Press. Originally appeared in the book *Uganda: A Case Study in African Political Development* by Peter M. Gukiina.

enterprise, chartered in 1888 by the British royal government. In 1893, the company's administrative function in Uganda was taken over by a British commissioner, and a year later the Kingdom of Buganda was placed under a formal British protectorate. This protectorate was extended in 1896 to cover most of what is now known as Uganda.

Britain ruled Uganda until October 1962, when Uganda achieved independence. The first constitution allowed for a federation in which Buganda and other kingdoms retained much autonomy. Dr. Milton Obote became the first prime minister under this system. In 1966, a new constitution was promulgated depriving the kingdoms of their previous autonomy and giving wide powers to Obote, who became president. The kingdoms were technically abolished and the country was divided into districts. On January 25, 1971, Obote was deposed by Idi Amin, who proclaimed the Second Republic of Uganda.

The people of Uganda are divided into four major racial groups—Bantu, Nilotic, Nilo-Hamitic and Sudanic. There are about thirty distinct tribes. The largest single ethnic group is the Baganda with more than one million members.

The majority of Uganda's eleven and a half million people are Christian. A small percentage, about 6 percent, are Moslem. The population is largely rural, growing coffee, cotton, and tea, which are the main exports. Some copper is mined and exported, and manufacturing, up until a few years ago, was expanding to create products for local consumption such as canned goods, shoes, fertilizers, cement, and steel. The economy, however, has been shaken by the expulsion of the Asians and the elimination of many of the educated and skilled black Ugandans. Because of the fear engendered by Amin's brutal reign of terror, many professional Ugandans have also fled. Four hundred Ugandan doctors are now living in exile.

When we came to Uganda, there were over 45,000 people of Indian, Pakistani, and Bengali origin living in the country. These people were referred to as ''Asians'' and comprised a visible minority, especially in the urban areas.

Yet history records that minorities often become scapegoats for tyrannical leaders. Many dictators have had a number of scapegoats—the intellectuals, foreigners, and the Jewish people. Amin, too, has used scapegoats hoping to satisfy, in part, the demands and needs of the Ugandan people. Israel was the first scapegoat. Accusing the Israelis of milking the economy, he quickly dispatched their technicians, army officers, and diplomats, declaring an all-out war on Zionism. The people were led to believe that once the country was rid of the Israelis and remained vigilant against Zionist subversion, Uganda would once again be on the road to prosperity.

A little more than a year later, Amin needed another solution to prove to the people that he was effecting some improvement in their lives. The economy was not improving. He was squandering far too much money on military hardware and personnel. There was also a great deal of corruption. In early August 1972, he found his scapegoat. He announced that according to the dictates of his dream, all Asians who were not Ugandans would be required to leave Uganda within three months. At face value, the decree was a blatant racist act, for it discriminated against certain foreigners by race. In effect, the decree, as it was carried out, was a flagrant disregard of the right to nationality. Asians who were clearly citizens of Uganda were arbitrarily told that they were no longer considered Ugandans. In ninety days, most of the brown-skinned Asian people had been thrown out of Uganda at the whim of a racist dictator.

Again, when the decree was first announced, diplomats—and even the Asians themselves—did not quite believe it. They thought it was another hoax to pressure the British.

Many believed that the first Asians came to East Africa as indentured laborers imported by the British to build the railroad from the Kenyan coast to Lake Victoria in Uganda. Actually, the link between East Africa and India has existed for centuries. Trade was carried on between these areas as early as three centuries before Christ. Indian beads, weights, and measures found on the African coast have been linked to the Hindus of Southeast India during the eighth to twelfth centuries. When the Portuguese gained control of the East African ports, they used Indian accountants and bankers. In the eighteenth and nineteenth centuries, when the Arabs dominated the East African coast, Indian

73

traders prospered. The Sultan in Zanzibar put Indians in charge of much of the financial administration of his government. In 1970, virtually all foreign trade passed through the hands of Indians.

While most of the Indians stayed in Zanzibar and the coastal towns, a few ventured into the interior in caravans. As the British gained a foothold in East Africa, they claimed authority over the Indian traders whom they considered subjects of the British Empire in India.

It was indeed the building of the railroad that brought large numbers of Asians into the interior of East Africa. Yet, they were not laborers. The statistics kept for the construction of the East African railroad show that less than 20 percent of the laborers remained in Africa. Most of the Asians who came to settle in East Africa came as free immigrants. While the railroad was being built, small communities of Indian traders sprang up around the work camps. Some of these traders came from families who had been doing business on the East African coast for generations. Others were attracted by the new economic opportunities opening up as the railroad advanced.

In 1914, there were approximately 3,000 Asians in Uganda. They were mostly retail and wholesale traders. They had not been encouraged to settle on the land, for the British viewed the Ugandan Protectorate as primarily an African territory, and thus land was not parceled out to the whites, nor to the Indians, for ownership. Thus, the Asians who came to Uganda came as traders, a tradition well established on the East African coast even before the birth of Christ. The retail and wholesale traders in turn attracted Indian artisans and craftsmen—carpenters, mechanics, shoemakers, tailors, and the like.

The Asians were the middlemen—between the British colonists and the Africans. They were economically useful to both the British colonists and the Africans, for they became a vital catalyst for economic development in the country. Asian traders introduced many to a cash economy, and they established grassroots businesses which the British had no desire to undertake. In the colonial period, the top positions were reserved for British and other European whites. The Asians had no hope of ever achieving the same status. Restricted in their upward mobility, the Asian minority carved out an economic niche for themselves as merchants, small businessmen, wholesalers, and craftsmen. Some prospered; most led a simple but comfortable life. All, however, had to work hard to obtain and keep that comfortable life.

However, the Asian community felt the sting of discrimination. They were never accepted on the same level as the British, even when they were given British protective status and the right to hold a British passport. The fact is, the Asians never had a privileged position; and if they believed they had one, they were foolish. Their schools were inferior, often supported by their own savings, and staffed by unqualified teachers. Most Asians were forced to seek higher education in India. When they returned, the Indian degrees were considered inferior by both Africans and Britons who had been educated in England. The Asians were never allowed to enter the British club.

When the political winds in the late 1950s changed and Africans rose to take up political leadership, the Asians lost whatever "middle" status there was. On paper, the racially stratified colonial society had been transformed into a democratic society devoid of racial distinctions and separatism. Asians were given a choice: apply for British protected status, entitling the person to a British passport, or become a citizen of Uganda. The majority of Asians applied for British protection. Yet a large number applied for Ugandan citizenship. In the 1969 census, over 26,000 Asians claimed to be Ugandan. Many Asians, however, charged that government officials dragged their feet in processing Asian citizenship applications, and as many as 30,000 applications were never processed.

The Asians who scorned the offer of Ugandan citizenship feared being members of a mistrusted minority in a nation struggling for unity. Many said, "What good is a piece of paper claiming citizenship if we are considered foreigners in the eyes of Africans?"

It is true that the relationship between Asian and African was indeed strained. We had traveled many times to Africa and had witnessed much prejudice between both groups. The reputation of Asians among the African populace was that of shopkeeper.

While certainly not all Asians were shopkeepers, the image of the Asian as small retailer still prevails today in the minds of most Africans. The shopkeeper was credited with opening up the remote areas of East Africa to trade, but he also bore the brunt of local criticism. The Indian shopkeeper was accused of fixing scales, misleading customers, shortchanging, and other forms of cheating. Undoubtedly, there was some substance to these complaints, yet they were often exaggerated.

Contact between Africans and Indians was sporadic and quite limited before the colonial period and there was hardly any intermarriage. General Amin capitalized on this attitude when he addressed a group of "citizen Asians" in 1972, saying, "You must come out and identify yourself with Ugandan Africans. . . . I want to see Africans marrying Asians and vice versa."

The Asian minority provided many economic breakthroughs for Uganda. They excelled in business—for that was their only outlet. They were not from the landed aristocracy; they had no political base; they had no political opportunities for advancement. Their only channel was business and industry. Some were creative in experimenting with new production techniques and invested freely in new opportunities. These Asians formed an important element in the rapidly growing industrial sector of the Ugandan economy.

The Asian presence was especially apparent in the cities. This was certainly true of Kampala. We had always enjoyed visiting Kampala and had looked forward to living there. It was not a sterile, modern complex thrust into an African setting. It had grown in parts, each having its special flavor. The king of Buganda had his palace. The tombs of the *kabakas* or kings were still preserved. Their meticulously woven thatched roofs swooped to a point high above the straw-laden floors below, lending a cathedral-like silence to the sacredness of the earth below where royal attendants continually watched over the remains of their dead kings.

The colonial era of Kampala was very much evident in the arched and pillared windows of the old Imperial Hotel and the once exclusive British Kampala Club. Modern office and government buildings were a mark of the newly independent state.

Woven through all of these elements were endless rows of small shops. Nestled behind long wooden porches, the doors of these shops remained open from early morning to sundown. Inside, saried women and turbaned men bustled behind counters and in front of long walls of shelves while they chattered back and forth to customers in Swahili or an Indian dialect. Walking through these streets was always an exhilarating experience. Spices twinged our noses, and the whir of sewing machines buzzed in our ears. The vivid colors of silks and cottons dazzled our eyes as shoppers laden with packages jostled to and fro along the wooden porches. Carefully lettered signs bore names like "Patel" and "Desai," "Bombay Emporium" or "Hassan's Bazaar." Kampala had a cosmopolitan flair.

The dominance of the Indian commercial enterprises in the urban areas, as well as the tiny towns in the outlying areas, bothered many of the African Ugandans. The Asians, in fact, were accused of forming a monopoly on trade and business. It was very difficult for an enterprising African to break into the trade market. Asians had a tendency to give their business only to Asians. Asians who held positions as clerks or assistants in foreign-owned firms or in embassies, banks, or even in certain civil service positions in the Ugandan government tended to steer orders for services toward their friends and relatives in the Asian community.

For example, in the U.S. Embassy we had several Asians. One controlled a great deal of the purchasing and maintenance. Whether it was a question of servicing an automobile or buying a new carpet, the Asian assistant would contact the Asian doing business in this area. Only after insisting on several bids, or contacting the firms directly were we able to give occasional orders to an African printer or a European furniture dealer. We were somewhat surprised by this, but we knew from living in other countries that favoring one's own relatives and members of one's own ethnic group in business transactions was not unusual.

There were a few successful Asian businessmen who clearly saw the need for a more equitable business relationship between the Asian and African people. Jayant Madhvani, the leading Asian industrialist in Uganda, for example, tried several schemes to encourage African participation in industry. One of these was a profit-sharing plan; another was a policy of making loans to Africans to start new businesses. The Madhvani group also entered into several partnerships with Africans and employed African managers of subsidiary industries.

We drove out to the Madhvani estate near Jinja one afternoon for lunch. Jayant Madhvani had died of a heart attack in 1971, a year before we arrived in Uganda; and, therefore, we had never met him. We had heard a great deal about his business enterprises and were anxious to see the estate where his father had come to carve out his business early in this century.

The estate was lush. Sugar grew high and strong in the fertile soil under the African sun. There was a compound of Madhvani family houses, each colorful, bright, and open to the African landscape. Everything was neatly organized on the estate—workers' homes, a school, clinic, a network of roads, and the sugar works themselves. We were impressed by the forward-looking business approach of the family.

The original Madhvani estate had grown into an industrial empire of over seventy companies. In Uganda, they had fifty-five factories employing 2,100 Ugandans. The family had become extremely affluent, but they saw no need to rest. They considered themselves Ugandans. Jayant Madhvani had served without pay in a government position under Obote. Most of their investment was in Uganda. They had a stake in its future. The ashes of both Jayant and the founding father of the Madhvani family had been scattered on the shores of Lake Victoria—they had never intended to leave Uganda. When the edict of expulsion was announced, they did not at first believe that it was meant for them. However, during the invasion of September 1972, the eldest of the family, Manubhai Madhvani, was arrested. The family feared for his life, for he had been taken to Makindye—the dreaded military prison. Andrew Torchia, an American journalist, who was imprisoned with Madhvani, wrote that the Asian industrialist was always cheerful and dignified, helping to keep up the spirits of those in the cell. Madhvani escaped the worst. He was brought to Amin, who informed him that he was not a citizen of Uganda. Madhvani was forced to leave the country.

Despite all the good will and energies of a number of Asian businessmen, the prevailing image of the Asian was the *dukawalla* or shopkeeper. We were aware of alienation between Africans and Asians in East Africa, and therefore, we really did not expect to see much sympathy for the Asian plight among the African masses.

To the African masses, the *dukawalla* was still a foreigner whose ways were strange. In the more remote areas, Africans were eager to buy and sell at the Asian store, but they felt that the Asian trader did little work to earn all the money he collected. The Africans toiled in the fields and suffered from drought. They walked many miles leading cattle to water and pasture grounds. While they sweated and labored, what did this Asian man do besides sit in his store and bargain?

Actually, Asian shopkeepers lived hard and isolated lives. They opened their shops early and continued buying and selling until late at night. Their families worked along with them and their homes consisted of a few rooms next to the shop. They operated on very thin margins, and carried all sorts of figures in their heads in order to calculate the exact price of each item.

It was tedious work. Often the store would be filled with a steady stream of visitors asking to see this or that, but only a few would actually buy, and often it was only a bar of soap or a few envelopes. The petty exchanges produced a few pennies here and there to be carefully amassed. It took years and a great deal of discipline for these shopkeepers to save enough money to invest in larger stocks or another store. There were very few personal indulgences. Most of the money went into expanding business opportunities.

But the shopkeeper and his family irked their African neighbors, especially by their social exclusiveness. Accustomed as they were to a class system, Asians tended to look upon their relationships with Europeans and Africans alike as permanent divisions. While they aspired to many of the material advantages of the Europeans, they still maintained their social and marital exclusiveness. To the African, this exclusiveness was manifest in the Asian's everyday dealings. Africans who worked for Asians often complained about the cold and insulting ways of the Asian.

They found the shopkeeper's manners gruff and sharp. The shop-keeper hardly had time for a kind word and was terribly overpowering and efficient.

Margaret can remember several American women from the Midwest who complained to her about the way they were treated at an Asian shop. Margaret had not been bothered by it. She was accustomed to being treated in the same manner at similar shops in New York. Obviously we had become accustomed to the rather chilly ways of New York businessmen and saw no difference among the Asian shopkeepers of Kampala!

Among the masses, the Africans did not understand the Asians nor did the Asians comprehend their African neighbors. Asians complained about the Africans being lazy. They did not understand why they could not produce more. Some ridiculed the African who received an education, mostly on scholarship, and then landed a plush government job that paid well and required little effort. Others became particularly incensed by the existence of corruption in government. Having been pressured into giving bribes and payoffs for licenses and permits, many Asians believed that African politicians could only be expected to exploit their people.

The African, on the other hand, saw the Asian—particularly those who had sought British protected status—as draining the economy of Africa. They saw Asians use devious methods of transferring money out of Uganda. In our travels throughout Africa, we would frequently be approached by an Asian asking us to facilitate the transfer of money. A favorite method was selling something to a European or American in exchange for a personal check in U.S. currency to be sent directly to the Asian's overseas bank account.

There was indeed deep alienation. The Asian small businessmen were no different from any other minority group involved in trade. It seems to be a worldwide phenomenon to distrust and dislike the small trader particularly when the trader is a member of a racial or ethnic minority. The Chinese in Southeast Asia, the Lebanese in parts of Africa and Asia, and the Armenians have all been accused of the same self-protecting attitudes.

The situation of the Asians in Uganda seemed very similar to that of the Jews of Germany. Jews were and still are accused of exclusiveness, for they are intent on maintaining the traditions of their Jewish religion. The particular concern of Jewish parents over the choice of a Jewish marriage partner for their children can be compared to the care of Hindu Asians in arranging for the marital future of their offspring. Jews were ridiculed for their different social and religious ways, just as the Asians were considered foreigners. Only now in the U.S. are we beginning to see the value of the Jewish tenacity in preserving the Jewish religious and cultural heritage. Finally, the predominant image of the Asian is the *dukawalla*. For the Jew, the image was the small merchant whose most often cited crime was petty cheating. It was this image of the dishonest Jewish merchant that was exaggerated and exploited by Hitler. It was the same image of the aloof, cheating Asian shopkeeper that Amin used to fool the people into accepting his expulsion of the Asian minority.

The weekend of Amin's announcement of the expulsion edict in August 1972, passed quietly. The Asians hoped that Amin was just bluffing, but as the next work week began, it became apparent that he was dead serious. The high commissioner from Great Britain, Richard Slater, was asked by Amin to facilitate the departure of all Asians entitled to British passports. As with many decisions of Amin, the expulsion order was not thoroughly thought out. Consequently, Amin issued a series of statements amending the order. On August 22, it was announced that Asians with Ugandan passports would be allowed to stay. However, the announcement was qualified by Amin's promise to "weed out all those who got their citizenship through corruption or forgery."

The British High Commission, which is equivalent to an embassy in commonwealth countries, brought extra staff to deal with the problems of the exodus. Preparations for departure were long and tedious. Every emigré had to fill out several forms, have the necessary doctor's certificates and the required inoculations, and finally arrange to pay the air fare. All properties and businesses were registered in the hope that someday their owners would be compensated for what they left behind. They were only permitted to take some personal belongings and a mere 50 pounds (almost $120). Long lines appeared in front of the British high commissioner's office. Asians waited, documents in hand, from early morning to late at night. "Why should we wait in line and fill out so many forms in order to be allowed to go to England?" many thought. "We have British passports. Why are not all British passport holders treated in the same way?" According to the official British attitude, Britain had a responsibility for its "colored" subjects, but it did not want to take them right away and all at once. Amin, however, demanded that the British take the responsibility for these people who claimed to be British and arrange for their departure immediately. It was a hard pill to swallow, but the British government had no choice.

We remember picking up the *Uganda Argus*, the daily newspaper, and reading advertisements placed by various English towns and communities. The message of these ads was, "Don't come here. We are already overcrowded."

As the weeks wore on, Asians who thought they were Ugandan citizens were asked to check on their status. Many were told that their papers were not in order or that they had made application for citizenship after the deadline. Some officials blithely tore up the papers in front of the desperate Asians.

The diplomatic community became alarmed. The right of citizenship was being arbitrarily taken from a group of people who happened to be of another race and culture. Protests were made, but it had no effect. Britain appealed to other countries for assistance in aiding these Asians that were rendered stateless. Canada was the first nation to come to their rescue. Other European and some Latin American countries followed. I sent a number of telegrams back to Washington requesting that a special immigration quota be opened for Ugandan Asians.

The situation had become even worse. Fear had spread among the Asian community and rightly so. Ugandan soldiers searched the departing Asians completely and repeatedly. If an Asian was found with more money than allowed, not only was the money taken by the soldiers but he was often beaten mercilessly. Jewelry with precious stones was confiscated. Some women were forced to remove all clothing during the searches, and there were several reports of rape. One woman was taken off the plane at Nairobi

These were among the first Asians to leave after Amin's expulsion. Like most Asians, they left with only small amounts of luggage.

and hospitalized after having been raped five times on the road from Kampala to the airport in Entebbe.

When the British government brought the matter of maltreatment before the United Nations, the Ugandan representative assured the world body that Ugandan soldiers and police would be stationed on the airport road to prevent any mishandling of the departing Asians. This was ludicrous. The entire diplomatic community in Kampala knew that the soldiers were responsible for the mistreatment and abuse. They had taken advantage of the situation to loot and steal from the Asians who had no way to defend their rights.

Asians who were leaving for India and Pakistan took the train from Kampala to Mombasa, Kenya. The soldiers inspecting these trains were particularly harsh. Many people were beaten, stoned, and robbed of even the mere 1,000 shillings they were permitted to take. Some were stripped naked and made to crawl through the train.

Even Asians who were Ugandan citizens panicked. Many wished to leave and went from embassy to embassy hoping to find someone to take them. By the end of September, halfway through the ninety-day period for departure, the United States government had not acted on a special quota for Asians. Asians knocked desperately on the embassy doors; but I had to tell them that I could only take applications in certain preference categories, and these would not be guaranteed entry. A mere seventy-seven Asians were granted visas under the normal immigration regulations.

On October 1, I sent a telegram to Washington. The telegram was addressed to the State Department, but I sent copies to the White House and to the Department of Justice to assure maximum coverage of my recommendation. We were at that point worried about reducing the numbers of American citizens living in Uganda, because of the deteriorating security. This was my concern. However, at the end of the telegram I warned that certain groups and nationalities would criticize the U.S. government severely for its inaction on the matter of the Ugandan Asians who were stateless. In other situations, we had been proud that the United States was always one of the first to respond to humanitarian needs. Those who are not familiar with our government and its tedious system of checks and balances cannot understand why it sometimes takes so long for our government to act. We grew impatient. Finally on October 2, the State Department announced that the U.S. government would open one thousand places for heads of families.

The State Department sent a specialist in counselor work to help us begin processing visas in a few days. Some embassy wives agreed to work full-time on the clerical staff. Others volunteered on a part-time basis. In addition, Margaret looked for ways to ease the plight of the Asian families. She organized a hospitality committee of twenty American women to assist those who were waiting long hours. Observing how Asians had been forced to wait in long lines in the hot African sun, she was determined, despite the U.S. government's tardy reply, to make the process as dignified as possible. She decided to use the hallway and the waiting room in the embassy for the hospitality center. The American women were as cheerful as possible. They joked about serving iced tea which was completely alien to the Asians, who were used to drinking their tea hot. Sometimes Margaret would tease them saying that they had to change their tastes if they intended to go to the States to live. It was a small effort, which only eased our guests temporarily. The pain and loss still remained in the eyes of our frightened applicants.

The effort of the American women was tiny indeed compared to the hurdles which the Asian people had to face. Margaret felt that although it was insignificant, at least it gave the American women a chance to help others in need. Because of the difficult political and security situation, Americans could not readily help our Ugandan friends. Curiously enough, however, when we arrived home and settled in Philadelphia in 1974, we met a large community of former Ugandan Asians. Margaret was surprised and heartened when many told her that the iced tea and the friendly atmosphere in the U.S. Embassy in Kampala had been such a contrast to the treatment they had been given elsewhere that they remembered it well. We still joke about the iced tea but we have not seen many conversions among the Asians to the drink.

To eliminate some of the risks of traveling to the airport, the various embassies and the United Nations office organized caravans from Kampala to Entebbe. We were assured that the Asians arrived safely at the airport terminal, but they were still subject to extensive searching at customs. As the deadline for the expulsion of the Asians drew closer, the mountains of crates and bundles of personal belongings appeared on the pavement outside the cargo building. It was all to be shipped when space on planes was available but much of it never arrived at its destination.

When we first came to Kampala, we noticed that the Asian families made a practice of walking together at sunset. Every evening, hundreds of Asian families would stroll along the streets and hillsides of Kampala. The gaily colored saris of the women flowed in the breeze, the men chatted enthusiastically, and the children skipped along with their playmates. The ritual suggested the inner peace of the Hindu East. The day's labor had been completed, the midday heat had disappeared, the sun was sinking, and dusk brought comfort and rest.

As the days wore on during that ninety-day period, the evening stroll was abandoned, for there was no longer any cause for comfort and peace. Instead, long lines of Asian men crowded the sidewalks in front of the office buildings of the city each day. They waited patiently in the blazing sun confused and bewildered about their future.

Most of the Asians did not vehemently protest when their papers, certifying their Ugandan citizenship, were torn up before their eyes. Many did not even question the officials of the British High Commission when they were told afterwards that they were not considered British passport holders. They patiently filled out forms and went from door to door—from the Canadian office, to the United Nations headquarters, to the U.S. Embassy—until they obtained the necessary visas. Many families were split with some going to Britain and others being admitted into other countries.

The women painstakingly packed whatever belongings they were allowed to take, sold what they could, and tearfully left home. The Asians submitted to detailed searches. Sometimes they were roughly treated, cursed, and beaten. An Asian hand was never raised in defense. There was anger and frustration but never violence. Perhaps their resignation is a part of the self-control of the Hindu culture; or was it because they felt so powerless to change the situation, and, therefore, did not even try?

We had heard and read many historical accounts of how the Jews marched to their death in the horror chambers of the Nazi prisons. The meekness of these victims of the holocaust as they met their fate is now ever present in the minds of the Jewish people. Today, Jews cry that they will never again suffer that fate. The Asians in Uganda did not suffer death. Yet they were driven from their homes and, for many, from the country of their birth.

Britain reluctantly helped those to whom it had a clear commitment based on their colonial past. Yet, as the first flights were being organized, British townspeople were making sure that the latest of refugees would not settle in their areas.

India, from which many had emigrated a long time ago, did little to help the Asians. Clearly those who had maintained their Indian and Pakistani passports were permitted to return, but for the stateless, even the homeland of their grandfathers turned its back. Only after continued efforts did other countries, including the U.S., come to their aid. The Asians were truly unwanted. They had no one to turn to for help. No one cared. Thus, they met their fate with resignation.

We recall how Amin carefully planned his assault on the Asian community. In 1971, Amin had forced all Asians to submit to a census count. He also cancelled the applications of about twelve thousand Asians for Ugandan citizenship. In 1972, he placed restrictions on Asians. He warned them that if they held political meetings, it would be at their peril. In 1972, shortly before the expulsion order, Amin accused the Asians of "sabotaging the economy of the country."

The economy of Uganda was in trouble. Amin had spent over twice the amount budgeted for military spending in the fiscal year ending in July 1972. An official from the United Nations Development Program came to Kampala to discuss the organization's concern with the excessive military spending. Amin's minister of finance also warned Amin that reserves were dipping so low that Uganda soon would be unable to pay for any imports.

Amin merely answered, "Print more money."

Amin then had a brilliant idea; declare economic warfare. Thus, in August, he announced an "Economic War" that included the Asian expulsion as phase one. Amin claimed that it was "based purely on the Ugandan government's determination to rectify Uganda's economy by putting it in the hands of its nationals."

The economic achievements of the Asians had proved their downfall. Amin capitalized on African mistrust, jealousy, and resentment of those achievements. He broke an already festering sore and encouraged the spread of racial animosity. The Asian expulsion was a scapegoat for a floundering economy. It diverted the attention of the army as well as the people, and served to rally the people to a popular cause to which his name would be linked forever. It took people's minds off the disappearances and killings that had taken place. Amin's racist tactics of dealing with a mistrusted minority were indeed similar to those of Hitler toward the German Jews.

Most Asians made no kind of physical protest. If there was any kind of rebellion, it was the scheming on the part of some Asians to find loopholes in the system so that they could take out of the country as much of their property as possible. It was a game of wits in which some Asians sought revenge by reassuring themselves that the Ugandan soldiers were not going to profit as much as they imagined.

A number of Asians sold what they could and invested in household items and personal clothing to be shipped to London. At first, this method succeeded until more restrictions and delayed shipments thwarted the Asian efforts. Others used illegal means such as smuggling precious jewels in a hairdo or turban. Some succeeded, others did not. A few purchased around-the-world airline tickets for each member of the family hoping to cash in the ticket when they reached London. We had heard stories of how German Jews managed to escape from Hitler's tyranny with some of their assets. The flight of the Ugandan Asians was, in some ways, a replay of the Nazi expulsion of the Jews.

When they were leaving Uganda, the Asians looked back on

the homes they had built and the cars they had bought with the savings they had accumulated little by little over the years. They looked back at the tiny store that their grandfather had established; the one in which they had worked from the time they were able to count. So many hours of work, so many years of saving—was it worth it all?

The Ugandan Asians are a mirror of minority groups who are convenient victims of despots. The Turks found it useful to eliminate one and a half million Armenians between 1915 and 1917. Hitler, two decades later, needed to focus the anger of the German people on another minority, and he chose the Jews.

Amin found the hard-working, inward-looking Asians a convenient target. Sadly, as with the Turks and the Germans, the Ugandan people were unable or unwilling to protect the human rights of this minority group.

The Asians were, for the most part, alone in their difficult hours as other minority groups have been in man's tragic history. In a little more than ninety days, the Asian community was uprooted from Uganda.

When the deadline date was reached, a number of Asians remained. They had met the test of Ugandan citizenship and wished to stay. Before a rally of applauding Ugandans, Amin announced that he was about to have these remaining Asians transported physically to various districts in the rural areas where they would be given plots of land to cultivate. "Be kind and helpful to them," he cautioned the crowd, "and teach them ways to dig hard and seriously." That was enough to frighten most of those who remained into leaving.

We had feared the worst for the Asians. Knowing that Amin had not hesitated in destroying the lives of so many Ugandans, especially after the September invasion, we felt that he would not hesitate in eliminating the Asians. In October, Amin had already told of his admiration for Hitler. We dreaded the consequences if some "non-Ugandan" Asians remained beyond the deadline. It would be so easy for the soldiers to separate the brown Asians from the black Africans. To our relief, it did not happen.

How was it that this expulsion of the Asian minority, which

caused so many to become homeless, did not turn into another bloodbath? The Asians are a very orderly people. They are stoic in accepting their fate, hardly ever turning to violence. Yet, in the accounts of Nazi Germany, we saw the Jews separated from the rest of the population and finally annihilated without any mass revolt. Certainly there was no moral compunction on the part of Amin.

Amin saw, however, that he did not have to resort to bloodshed. He knew that his threats could rid Uganda of the Asians by forcing others into helping the destitute minority. As a result, Britain, India, and Pakistan all lived up to their responsibilities in effecting the exodus of their passport holders. Furthermore, other nations and international bodies finally joined hands to assist the stateless.

For Amin, it was a resounding success. In ninety days, practically all the Asians were gone, leaving houses, cars, bank accounts, stores, and factories. As soon as they were gone, Amin began to parcel out the plums. The Ugandan people were promised by Amin that the commercial interest of the country would at last be transferred into the hands of black Ugandans. They dreamed of seeing a bustling Kampala Road lined with thriving shops owned by Africans. The dream of overnight enrichment was, however, a sham. Amin appointed a committee to parcel out the shops left by the Asians. Most of them went to military officers and their families. Some of the shops themselves had been emptied, for the departing Asians sold all they could and never reordered before they left. At other shops, the new owners sold out the stocks before they had enough money to reorder. Hardly any of the new owners had any capital or credit on which to build a business. All they had was the key to a shop and its partially filled shelves. And with the Asians gone, there were far fewer people with capital to spend. A number of the shops and businesses had been supported exclusively by Asian clientele. We remember a few flower shops in Kampala. Asian families used flowers extensively in their homes. Sending and giving flowers was a frequent social custom among the Hindus. The flowers sold at the shops were grown by African Ugandans. One flower supplier was a self-help community group outside of

Kampala. When the Asians left, there were no more buyers. Thus, the flowers went unsold. The source of income for the self-help project had evaporated. The group changed over to growing some vegetables, but then it was impossible to find fertilizer and insecticide. Some small American assistance had been given to the self-help project, and from time to time, American women had volunteered their services.

One such project had consisted of a community center where various youth and nursery school programs were held. It had been started by an older Ugandan woman who owned a bar in the area. After her children had grown and her husband retired, she had second thoughts about her life. She began to ask herself "What have I done for my people except fill them with liquor?" She sold the bar and bought the property to establish the center. She dedicated her whole life to it, influencing others to volunteer their time and money. The Asian departure and the collapse of the Ugandan economy hurt the project deeply.

In October and November, shops were boarded up until they were transferred to African hands. Food supplies were always available while we were there, but other items were sometimes scarce. We recall that at one time we could not find a needle or pin in Kampala. These items had to be ordered from Nairobi, Kenya.

With the sudden departure of the Asians, there was no one to take the place of skilled workers in the factories. Many industries collapsed—the sugar industry was a prime example. The plantations of the two leading Asian families had begun to export sugar overseas. In fact, it was Jayant Madhvani who negotiated a sugar quota for Uganda. Even now, the sugar refineries cannot even produce enough sugar for local consumption. People stand in line for sugar rations, and many resent the fact that the military have first choice.

The situation with the foreign exchange grew so grave that the government had to prohibit the importation of many items. Some of the decisions were made in an arbitrary fashion with little regard to long-term planning. For instance, we saw the collapse of a U.S. sponsored chicken cooperative. The project had just about reached the last stage of development, during which a hatchery would be built and staffed. Until the hatchery was constructed, baby chicks had to be imported and given out to various farmers. The chicks were then raised on special feed and returned to the cooperative where the grown chickens were killed, cleaned, and frozen for sale. The project had been very successful. It was being run by Ugandans and it produced plump and delicious chickens. Uganda even obtained a contract to export frozen chicken to eastern Zaïre. During the foreign exchange crunch, the baby chicks were prohibited, and the project collapsed.

Amin's Economic War has been a total disaster. He has employed Egyptians, Libyans, Palestinians, and other Arabs to fill technically skilled positions. He has even invited back Indians on specific contracts. The temporary importation of skilled workers has not, however, worked. They have no stake in the country. It is the same as employing mercenaries to fight a war. Amin's response to his economic plight has been described as "offering the people circuses instead of bread."

As for the Ugandan Asians who have left, they have resettled in countries like Britain, Canada, and the U.S., attempting to start from scratch as many other immigrants have done in the past. Just as many of the Jews who fled Germany did, Ugandan Asians who have come to the United States are beginning life again. They have found jobs—even the women—but they feel alone. There is no large Asian community in which to socialize. Some sadly complain, "The family is dispersed. They have gone their separate ways." Many, however, are saving money to open their own businesses, for trading is their livelihood. They still look longingly back to their homes in Uganda bewildered and sometimes bitter over their plight. One Ugandan Asian who settled in New Jersey suddenly picked up the phone and rang his house in Kampala. A voice answered the call and he shouted into the receiver, "What the hell are you doing in my house!"

In some ways, Amin has been typical of past brutal tyrants. Like Hitler, he first selected the Jewish community as the focus for his brutality. Within a few months after his takeover, he found that the Jews were a convenient group for him to brutalize. And again, the external world community responded to Amin in the same low-key ineffectual way that it did to Hitler.

The Asian community was the second group that Amin selected for his brutalization. In about one hundred days of threats and bombast, Idi Amin uprooted and deported the overwhelming majority of brown-skinned people in Uganda. The Asians were convenient scapegoats in 1972, as the Jews were in 1971, for his gross maladministration.

While the international community condemned both acts of brutality, the world did little to stop them. The man who praised Hitler and acted like him found little international opposition to his evil.

Consequently he continued his brutality.

6: IS AMIN AN AFRICAN HERO?

"I DO NOT WANT TO BE CONTROLLED BY ANY SUPERPOWER. I myself consider myself the most powerful figure in the world, and that is why I do not let any superpower control me"—Idi Amin.

After his successful coup, Amin believed himself to be a hero. In his simplistic way, he realized that being the hero would keep him in power. He began searching for ways to reinforce his hero image.

Amin succeeded first in gaining approval in Uganda. There had been a great deal of dissatisfaction with the government of Milton Obote. He had moved to the left by nationalizing eighty-five companies and the export-import trade. This socialist program left the management of these companies intact and the masses saw little change. Not only was Obote decidedly dull, but he did not produce any improvements for the common people he claimed to champion.

Amin was a refreshing change. In January 1971, when he staged his successful coup, he appeared before the people as one who would save them from the excesses of the Obote regime. He promised free elections. He released the political prisoners. He set up a temporary alliance with the Baganda people, who had been oppressed and neglected under Obote. Amin, however, owed his success to a military faction composed of his own tribal members; the Kakwa and other Nubians whom he had personally recruited and promoted. With Baganda brains and Kakwa and Nubian brawn, Amin was ushered into the Ugandan presidency. He learned to savor the taste of power, and soon heads were smashed and bodies were severed and tossed into the Nile River. Amin's despotic rule turned on practically every tribal group. In the end, Amin could trust no one, not even the members of his own Kakwa clan. His army is now a mercenary army composed of Ugandan and Sudanese Nubians whose loyalty is assured by the lucrative pay, luxuries of command, and the spoils of Amin's economic war. A number of southern Sudanese, having amassed small fortunes in Uganda, have retired to the Sudan to live a comfortable life.

From the point of view of foreign interest, Britain was definitely pleased with Obote's overthrow. Obote's socialist gestures and his courting of the Soviets and the Chinese made Britain look to the military officer, Idi Amin, to return to the *status quo*.

For a while it seemed as though Amin could emerge as an African hero. First of all, he is a Kakwa, a tribe in Uganda which comprises less than 1 percent of the entire Ugandan population. The Kakwa people live in a corner of Uganda on the very tip of the West Nile region bordering on both the Sudan and Zaïre. Except for some of the northernmost areas of Acholi and Karamoja, it is about the furthest one can be from the Ugandan capital. Remote and distant, the people of the West Nile were indeed a forgotten group.

Amin is from peasant stock. When he first gained power, he claimed to be a man of few words, but he soon learned to speak. His oratory pleased him, for he knew that he could sway a crowd, and make them laugh and stand in awe. Diplomats and the educated elite of Uganda were embarrassed by Amin's poor English. His grammar was almost always incorrect and his vocabulary earthy. He did not know the finer terms of diplomacy or governmental phrases. Neither did he know the current rhetoric of African nationalism. The ordinary people, however, were attracted to him. His phraseology was much like their own. They felt close to him because he used simple words that they could understand. Previous Ugandan leaders had been accustomed to fancy sayings and complicated sentences. Here at last was someone who spoke on their level.

Occasionally, Amin would read a speech from a prepared text. We remember being in the audience at an official ceremony in Kampala and watching diplomats and Ugandan officials squirm as Amin would mispronounce and stumble over words. People would sit on the edge of their chairs mentally wishing that they could help him along like a school child reading aloud in front of a class. He was a complete bore during those speeches, but as soon as he had finished, he would launch into his extemporaneous remarks. People nodded off the drowsiness and turned their full attention to Amin. The common people enjoyed these moments and listened carefully, for often, although his English was poor, his language was colorful and his imagery unique. One time he

95

turned to students at the University of Makerere and began his informal remarks with, "Now I have got a couple of rockets for you."

Although Amin's language was very close to the masses, he instinctively placed himself above their level. He did this through the tone of a schoolmaster or local chief, for most often he would be giving the people advice, or upbraiding them for their behavior. The most distinctive feature of his manner of speaking was his hand gestures. He would spread his fingers wide and show his palms to the crowd. At each oratorical point, Amin would curl his fingers back and push his palms forcefully toward the audience. It reminded us of vaudeville singers of the past such as Eddie Cantor or Al Jolson, who would flash their white-gloved hands in front of their blackened faces as they danced across the stage.

Amin was noted, too, for remaining in touch with the troops. He often would spend evenings drinking and telling jokes in the barracks with the ordinary soldiers. They enjoyed his familiarity and were flattered by the ease in which Amin fraternized with his men.

One weekend, all the diplomats were asked to be present at the opening of a new hotel in the southern part of Uganda. In the evening, crowds of local people came to dance and enjoy the music. The President mingled among them, seemingly without protection. As the evening wore on, Amin's energy seemed to increase. He seemed boosted by the gaiety of the people. As diplomats slipped away to get some sleep, the celebration continued into the wee hours of the morning.

It was difficult for us to be enthusiastic about any festivity. With all the blood that was being shed, how could people genuinely celebrate anything? We knew that sometimes in human history, song and dance were ways to make life bearable in times of stress. The slaves bore unbelievable injustice. Yet the only way they could live in a hopeless world was to escape from the cruelty of the present through song and dance.

But how could people be enthusiastic about celebrating with the man who was personally responsible for so much cruelty and sorrow? Undoubtedly, there were those who were forced into participating. An invitation from the President meant that they had to be present; and though they did not approve of what was taking place, they attended the official functions and pretended to be pleased with the occasion. We, after all, were there for the same reason. As diplomats accredited to Uganda, we were expected to appear at all official government functions to which we were invited. By October 1972, three months after our arrival we knew well the type of man we were dealing with and we took no pleasure in any of his celebrations.

We remember reading of the parades and festivities in Nazi Germany. People were stirred by martial music and in almost reflexive fashion would join in the goose stepping and saluting of marchers. Those who did not eagerly give the Nazi salute were automatically beaten.

By the time we left Kampala in 1973, fear had gripped the people of Uganda. The news of gross killings and atrocities far outweighed any benevolent attitudes or actions on the part of their self-chosen leader.

However, in the first year of his rule and even during part of the time we stayed in Uganda, many people truly felt attracted to him and hoped that somehow he would provide the leadership needed to unite a much divided country.

There were and still are many divisions in Uganda—ethnic, religious, and geographic. In the multiplicity of tribal groups there is a definite north-south pattern. In the north, people belong to the Nilotic and Nilo-Hamitic language groups. They come from a pastoral tradition. The tribes in the south belong to the Bantu language family. Many of these tribes were well organized kingdoms at the time of the arrival of the British in the nineteenth century. The Baganda tribe appeared to be the most numerous and most powerful. Through their *kabakas* (or kings), Britain formed an alliance with the Baganda. In this region on the shores of Lake Victoria, the British concentrated much of its colonial control and also benevolence. This was further reinforced by the presence of Christian missionaries who arrived in Buganda in 1875. As the colonial period gained momentum, the other Bantu tribes of the south prospered; and in the end, they received many more favors than the tribes of the north.

We had read a great deal about Uganda and its background

over the years. Most of the Ugandan students whom we had met in the United States were Baganda. Unlike many other African students at that time, they came from families that had been Christian for several generations. The parents of many of them had received some education. They were generally more "Westernized." On the other hand, they were deeply immersed in their own particular culture.

They extolled their own language, Luganda, and spoke of the long lines of *kabakas* who went back one thousand years. They were extremely interested in education and had an intellectual approach to success. Most were also of landed aristocracy. They possessed plots of land that had been in the family for long periods of time and they considered land a prime factor in their own economic future. In fact, we noticed that although the Baganda entered the civil service or took positions in banks and other business firms, they very often continued to hold onto large acreages of farm land. They quickly learned modern techniques, and through influential acquaintances obtained loans and equipment to transform the farms from the ordinary hand-plowed plots to efficient agricultural projects. With their extended family providing the manpower, they were able to work at desk jobs and maintain farms at the same time.

Britain used the highly centralized political kingdom of Buganda to extend its influence to the rest of Uganda. The *kabakas* were highly interested in expansion and thus cooperated with British designs. Gradually, the Baganda were used in various positions, such as tax collectors and local administrators in other areas throughout Uganda. Many other ethnic groups in Uganda had to learn and speak Luganda in order to do business or obtain justice. It was natural then for other tribes to resent the Baganda—for they represented foreign domination. Furthermore, the other tribes saw that they were being shortchanged. The region of Buganda possessed more modern roads, schools, and hospitals. It also contained the commercial and political capital. The other tribes wanted more of what the Baganda had.

Buganda makes up about one-fourth of the country in size. Its people are clearly the most numerous group in Uganda. Three years before independence, census figures indicated that while the Baganda constituted not quite 20 percent of the population, they made up 30 percent of the school population. Almost half of the students at the University of Makerere were Baganda. In 1962, the year of independence from Britain, the Baganda held three-quarters of all the civil service positions and made up about half of the educated elite. It is not surprising that other ethnic groups banded together to push the Baganda out of their privileged position.

Milton Obote was a Lango, a member of an ethnic group situated to the north of Buganda. The Langi had largely been pastoral people, herding animals rather than growing crops. They did not have the centralized form of hierarchical monarchy similar to Buganda. During the colonial administration, however, their society changed from pastoral to agricultural. They became the third largest cotton producing area in Uganda. Obote, however, was a member of the intellectual elite and, politically, he had to stake his future on the neutralization of Baganda power. He drew his support from several sources. Northerners who resented the economic and political power of Buganda, as well as the dominance of the other Bantu-speaking groups, looked to Obote in their struggle to equalize the opportunities for economic, political, and educational growth in their areas.

Obote also drew support from those other ethnic groups to the south who resented being dominated by the Baganda. And lastly, even among the Baganda, Obote attracted those who opposed the monarchists. They were mostly young educated Baganda who believed the traditionalist views were not consistent with the political structure of a modern state. On paper, in 1966, it seemed that Milton Obote had the perfect equation for ruling a complexity of ethnic groups and interests.

Why the equation of Obote did not succeed has been endlessly analyzed. We had met and interviewed Milton Obote in Kampala in the early 1960s, and followed with interest the Ugandan political scene. It became apparent that Obote's political base was eroding. He had been severe in his dealings with the monarchists of the south, who were shocked by the destruction of their political kingdom. Obote had forced the issue of centralized government and moved swiftly to form a one-party government.

Milton Obote, former president, ousted by Idi Amin in January 1971.

Two Ugandans are readied for execution by firing squad during early public executions in 1973.

The one-party state is certainly not unusual in Africa. Many countries have established this form of government. The reason advanced for the one-party form is that developing nations cannot afford time and money on parliamentary systems made up of several political parties. Furthermore, it is contended that multiparty government requires an educated populace attuned to sophisticated voting issues and procedures. Regardless of the merits of such systems, the one-party government is a fact of life in Africa. Most African countries have abandoned multiparty governments and are now being ruled by just one party which is either civilian directed or inspired by the military.

Obote's bid for transforming the country into a one-party state was resisted by several elements in Uganda, particularly the Baganda educated elite.

The key to his downfall, however, was the military. The composition of the Ugandan army was and still is a prime factor in the political power equation. First of all, the people of the south were never interested in the army. Among the Baganda, there existed adequate means for upward mobility, both through agricultural development and business opportunities, and most of all, through education, which was an instant ticket to a salaried position. In the north where educational opportunities were limited, the army offered a chance for betterment. During the colonial era, the British recruited large numbers from the north for several reasons. First of all, they knew that because it was a less privileged area, the people had more modest ambitions. The colonial army held only moderate prestige for Africans and limited possibilities for advancement. Only among the less advantaged were the British successful in finding recruits who would remain in the profession.

Second the army had height requirements. The Bantu people of the south tended to be too short, while the northerners were able to qualify. Moreover, the less educated were considered more malleable. They would answer "Yes, sir" without questioning.

Lastly, there was the colonial formula, "divide and rule," that is much quoted by Amin in his tirades against imperialism. Indeed in this case, Amin is correct. The British used army recruits from one area or ethnic group to police other areas and ethnic groups. This reinforced ethnic divisions and hatred. British officers knew that it would be difficult for members of a tribe to police their own members. Amin and his battalion were taken to Kenya to control the Mau Mau uprising largely among the Kikuyu of Kenya. The Kikuyu leaders of present-day Kenya often allude to this in their occasional spats with Amin. They denounce him as a traitor who worked against the nationalist cause in Kenya.

At the time of independence, the army in Uganda consisted of only one thousand men with little equipment. The army relied on British leadership, for it only had two African commissioned officers, one of whom was Amin. Five years later, the army had increased 400 percent to become the seventh largest on the continent. In 1964, the army struck for more pay. Instead of being disciplined, the army gained sizable increases, making it one of the most remunerative professions in Uganda.

As the army grew in leaps and bounds, the officers had to be trained on crash programs provided by different foreign nations. There was considerable internal fighting within the army. To control this powerful colossus, Obote applied the old formula of "divide and rule," playing one group against the other. He encouraged factionalism and attempted to prevent one person, namely Amin, from gaining complete control of the army. In addition, Obote promoted the recruiting of army soldiers among the Langi and Acholi tribes. In the meantime, Amin played along with the game doing his own recruiting in the extreme north among his own ethnic base, the Kakwa, and other Nubian tribes bordering the Sudan.

In the long run, it was just personal opportunism that drove Amin to stage a coup d'état. Obote was trying to thwart Amin's power. Amin was then army chief of staff. Before leaving for a conference in Singapore, Obote had set the stage for Amin's dismissal from the army, for Amin was being investigated on charges of misappropriation of funds. To save himself and his career, Amin decided to act. The fragmentation in the army succeeded in aiding Amin and his small coterie of Kakwa and Nubian soldiers. The grievances of various groups against Obote and his government aided in the success of Amin's coup.

Outside of Uganda, Amin was viewed with a great deal of

suspicion by African leaders. First of all, the civilian rulers of Africa were intensely fearful of military coups. They were reluctant to sanction them for they themselves were constantly threatened by their own armies and the power of the gun. Besides, Milton Obote had been a very acceptable member of the club of African leaders as he wrestled with the problems of development and searched for ways of severing some of the ties to the former colonial powers. As Amin became entrenched and as reports came indicating the support of the Ugandan people for Obote's removal, African leaders finally accepted him.

In February 1971, about a month after the coup, the Organization of African Unity met in Ethiopia. Both Amin and Obote (who was based in Tanzania), sent representatives. There was no agreement on which delegation should be seated. Obote had a number of friends among the progressive group of African leaders, but clearly, about a third of the African governments had come to power through coups similar to Amin's. Frustrated, the meeting adjourned. Amin had at least succeeded in preventing the Obote supporters from being seated at the meeting, but in the course of adjournment, the place for the OAU summit meeting of African heads of state was changed from the previously scheduled Kampala to Addis Ababa the capital of Ethiopia.

The fact that he had not been readily accepted bothered Amin. Some leaders, such as Julius Nyerere, president of Tanzania, and Kenneth Kaunda, president of Zambia, would have nothing to do with him. He began to plan a revenge. He wanted desperately to be considered a great African leader. Having served under Obote from the time of independence, he was vaguely familiar with the jargon of anticolonialism and liberation. He had not, however, studied anything about the economic or political intricacies of Uganda. He worked from experience and intuition. His former foreign minister, Wanume Kibedi, who later resigned and fled, described meetings of Amin's cabinet. At first, Kibedi said that Amin listened carefully to the analyses and advice of his ministers, most of whom were accomplished technicians. Gradually, however, he became bored. He could not grasp what his ministers had to say and found it a waste of time to consult with them. After a few months he began to make decisions on his own, shunning any advice.

Basically, he knew that he wanted to prove to his African colleagues that he was more of a liberator than anyone else. His first act of liberation for Uganda was to expel the Israelis. He knew, in very simple terms, that he could not be accused of being influenced by anyone. Next on his list were the Asians, whom he charged with "milking the economy." Several African leaders came to visit Amin during this period. The official excuse was to help mediate the dispute between Tanzania and Uganda, but the issue of the Asians was also included in the discussions. Both Mobutu Sese Seko, president of Zaïre, and William Tolbert, president of Liberia, arrived at Entebbe airport for official visits.

In the case of Mobutu, it was publicly known that there had been a misunderstanding. Mobutu evidently urged Amin to temper his decree on the Asians by at least postponing the date of the deadline. It was announced by the official press in Zaïre that Amin had agreed to extend the deadline. The next day, Amin denied it by asserting that he had "no intention whatsoever of extending it." Mobutu was indignant. He told the Zaïre News Agency in an interview that he continued to believe that he had been dealing with an honorable and conscientious statesman. He said, "I would be particularly sad if the facts should prove me wrong." The facts did prove him wrong. President Mobutu had either misunderstood Amin or had been deliberately misled.

With an almost peasant understanding, Amin realized that a king does not change his mind. What is written is written. For Amin, what is decreed is decreed. He saw that his expulsion order was working and there was no need to back down. Frankly, the Asian question was not just a Ugandan issue. It affected all of East Africa and parts of central and southern Africa. Different African countries had shown varying policies toward the Asian community, but most Africans agreed that Asian monopoly in certain commercial areas had to be broken in order to give the black Africans a chance. In Tanzania, a form of socialism was introduced in which private enterprise was vastly regulated and controlled. For example, the government set up agencies to control the importing and wholesale market. Housing was regulated whereby only the government owned hotels and large complexes while private ownership was permitted for only one residence per family. Many Asians were engaged in hotel and real estate businesses. As a result, many opted to leave once their holdings had been taken over by the state. In a sense, these moves were directed against Asians, and yet, they were not discriminatory. The rules and regulations applied to all Tanzanians and foreign aliens. Black Tanzanians were not given businesses and houses of departing Asians, nor were they permitted to own more than one house.

Even government officials found the regulations a hardship, for there were a number of them who had also invested in the same enterprises. One could argue that the Tanzanian majority, which was African black, chose to live a certain way, and therefore demanded that all Tanzanians or foreign aliens—regardless of race—abide by these decisions. As we have seen, this was not true in Uganda. A race was singled out and separated from the rest. Amin saw no use in devising complicated legal codes and systems to force the Asians out gradually. He did it with one thrust.

Some Africans actually approved of his action. He externalized many of the feelings of impatience and racial prejudice. They applauded his courage. No other leader had been so forthright in dealing with this problem which had plagued them for so many years. But some Africans made a distinction. They believed that those who were Ugandan citizens had been wronged by Amin. With regard to those who had remained under British protection, they thought Amin had been absolutely right.

African governments in East Africa had become impatient with Britain on the subject of the Asians. They had continually pressed London on the question and warned the British that they could no longer grant so many British Asians the same privileges of nationals. African governments forged ahead on Africanization programs. As more and more black Africans were trained, they squeezed Asians out of jobs. In some cases, Asians who had taken out citizenship in the East African countries complained that they were being denied their rights. This was a clear case of discrimination. Others who had British passports, however, had no recourse. African governments served Britain notice that they no longer needed the services of these aliens residing in East

105

Africa. Britain dragged its feet. In 1968, the British Labor government had passed a law limiting entry of Asian passport holders to three thousand a year, thus setting a convenient timetable for the British people to absorb them. At that rate, it would have taken forty years for all Asians with British passports to be cleared out of Uganda. The African governments objected. Forty years was too long for them. Nevertheless, most governments did not force the issue and instead exerted steady and persistent pressure to hurry along Britain's immigration policy.

Only Amin directly challenged the British on this matter. He flung the whole problem in their laps. He delighted in reports from Britain about local opposition to the latest brown immigrants invading the crowded British Isles. "The British are very worried," he declared. "I have taught them a lesson and that is why I am the best politician in the world."

Continuing his Economic War to put the Ugandan economy in the hands of Ugandans, Amin took over tea plantations and other businesses and farms owned by the British expatriates. The British government in turn canceled loan agreements and technical assistance programs and downgraded its official representation in Kampala.

Surprisingly, the official government newspaper of Tanzania commented on Amin's latest moves. It said that when Amin had come to power he was pro-South African, pro-British, pro-Zionist, and pro-imperialist. "But in recent months, General Amin's policy has experienced a significant shift. He no longer talks of visiting South Africa. What is more, he has taken over Anglo-American capitalist firms and plantations." The editorial continued to urge Amin to further nationalize but to socialize as well.

Some political analysts, both within and outside of the African continent, were beginning to think that Amin might emerge as an African hero. He had all the usual traits. He was from a disadvantaged tribe. He had not been Westernized by formal education, or by Christianity. He was rugged, colorful, and earthy, and seemed to possess natural-born qualities of leadership. His burly figure and toughness engendered fear and awe. His humor and comradeship were much liked by simple village folk.

Most of all, he had courage. He was not afraid to stand up to a superpower. He did not back down; he did not change his mind. He sent telegrams to heads of state and spoke frankly with them. He invited himself to visit European leaders, and was cordially received. No one had dared before to send the Asians to Britain in one thrust. No one had dared to turn the tables on the British so successfully. Intellectuals were embarrassed by him. Western diplomats called him unpredictable. The international press made a buffoon of him. Nevertheless, with his peasant shrewdness, Amin could possibly turn out to have the spirit necessary to rally other Africans behind him in his fight against the "superpowers." Amin himself analyzed his position, "It is very hard, but I like it very much. One must think and not be a coward. Very many Africans have written to me that I am the hero of Africa. This makes me very proud."

Literary and political portrayals of Zulu Chief Shaka popularly depict the heroic qualities of the South African leader who built a massive empire in the early 1800s. His bravery, as well as his cruelty, are well known subjects for history books as well as poetry. He is a legendary figure not only in southern Africa among the Zulu descendants, but throughout black Africa. The very name Shaka evokes pride and awe from both child and adult in Africa. Some saw Amin in the same tradition—a warrior, from an insignificant clan, with the same fearful charisma, shrewd mind, and teasing humor. According to the Christian author Mofolo, Shaka chose to kill the woman he loved to obtain the chieftainship. Amin, too, has sacrificed his wives. One was killed, another escaped death, and another has not been seen since Amin divorced her.

The issue of "propaganda" is a favorite topic of Amin's. The BBC, the British radio station, is particularly strong in East Africa. We listened to it faithfully, for it was one of the ways we could keep in touch with world news. Amin also listens and often he becomes furious with the reports on Uganda. In fact, he has now decreed that anyone caught listening to the BBC will be considered a traitor. Despite the threat, recent Ugandans who have fled have assured us that radios are still turned secretly to the BBC and other stations outside of Uganda. In a country such as

107

Uganda, where the newspaper, radio, and television contain so many blatant lies, radio contact with the outside world is a vital source of information. In fact, it is the only source other than word of mouth.

The daily English language newspaper, the *Uganda Argus*, was taken over by the government in December 1972, and called the *Voice of Uganda*. It had been owned by an English group, but staffed by Ugandans. Up until that time, the newspaper had been very careful in its reporting so as not to be accused of treason or subversion. After the government took over control, no critical faculty was left in determining the news.

When the newspaper changed hands, there was hardly a ripple of criticism from other countries—except Britain. Most governments in Africa own and control the media. They are controlled so as to "educate" the people and to insure that there is no criticism that is divisive. Even in areas with privately published newspapers, there are still controls. Freedom of the press is only known and appreciated in Western Europe, Canada, and the U.S. (and a few other countries). Americans have held it to be a sacrosanct right—so much so that some who lament the amount of pornographic material believe that we may have pushed this right and freedom a little too far. Freedom of the press is an issue on which there is no basic world agreement. In fact, we in the West are in a minority.

Some observers like to make comparisons between the village rulers of precolonial African history and Idi Amin. Much like the *kabakas* and warrior heros of the past, Amin rules by fear and cruelty. He is, they argue, part of the African tradition.

We never considered Idi Amin an African hero or a veritable African leader—traditional or otherwise. He is a misfit. We do not see any indication that Amin is rooted in African tradition. First of all, it is doubtful that he was brought up within a respected African tradition. Amin was supposedly born in Koboko County in West Nile. But Amin has confused the issue by saying on several occasions that he was born elsewhere. If he was born in West Nile, it is likely that he left at a very early age, perhaps even as a baby. The true facts of Amin's early background are kept a mystery. Amin says one thing and then contradicts it by another statement. Some claim that Amin's parents separated soon after his birth and that he moved with his mother to a community of Nubians who had been recruited to work on the sugar estates near Jinja.

Amin stayed with his mother in those early years as she moved from one place to another. Very little is known of Amin's father. A variety of sources indicate that no father was present in the early life of Amin.

The young boy Amin lived among the Nubian communities in the populated southern Bantu sections of Uganda. The workers at these communities were far from their original soil. They were somewhat like migrant workers who had abandoned their traditional setting to live and work in a cash economy quite different from that to which they had been accustomed. They lived as foreigners in another land. As time wore on, the ties to their traditions and culture weakened, but their ethnic loyalty grew even more intense as they banded together, separated from their Bantu neighbors. These groups of Nilotic tribes from the north were not liked by the Bantu tribes of the south. They were all classified as Nubians—the same people who had been employed by Lord Lugard when he subdivided the southern Bantu kingdoms of Toro, Bunyora, and Buganda in 1891. A taxi driver once told us that the Baganda used the term Nubian to call a person the very lowest of the lowly.

Amin, therefore, was not from peasant rural stock rooted to the land of his ancestors and steeped in the traditions of a much-neglected ethnic group. He was, rather, a member of an itinerant group of people who had left their native region to become migrant workers and soldiers. There was an almost mercenary mentality among these people. Amin came from a rootless family. True, the people had been oppressed and shortchanged, but he himself undoubtedly was affected, not by the rituals and spiritual beliefs of the tribal family, but by the mercenary attitude of the shiftless people with whom his mother associated.

Amin's entrance in the army was a major change in his life. Suddenly, he had purpose and discipline. His training as a recruit did not provide any depth. He was taught to obey commands and to shoot a gun. He was intensely committed to the army and became a fanatical soldier.

Amin probably witnessed continual violence as his mother shifted from place to place. In the army, violence became institutionalized for Amin. If there was a warrior tradition for Amin to follow it was the mercenary outlook of a small band of migrant Nubians. He went from the rough and tumble of a shiftless society to the barracks life of the King's African Rifles.

It is true that he exhibited a subservient attitude toward his British commanders. Because of this, they called him a good chap but remarked about his ruthless ways. As long as the British officers were in command, it did not matter. The British colonial army needed African recruits who were fearless. No attention was given to the human development of the soldier. Surely Amin noticed the prejudicial and condescending attitudes of some of his British officers. He was quite aware of the consequences of colonial rule and he resented it. But he cleverly concealed these feelings, which only now have been revealed to their full extent. He made the most of his situation playing the part of an exemplary soldier so that he would personally advance through the ranks.

Amin was and still is ambitious. He came from nothing. He cannot even claim to have had a traditional African background. We have never heard him speak of any significant childhood remembrances. He never mentions any ethnic rituals or customs. His actions seem to indicate that he has no knowledge of these customs. He thus cannot be considered an African hero stemming from the traditions of the past.

He was indeed a man who had risen from the dust of a simple mud hut to become a powerful military commander. It was his pure personal ambition which catapulted him into power. He embraced whatever point of view served his best interests. There was no consistency except brutality and his own fearlessness. The most important issue for him was to remain courageous. As a young recruit he would dash ahead of all the others. He will not admit defeat. Even after the Israeli raid, Amin remarked to the victors, ''As a professional soldier, I must tell you that the operation was very good. But you did not get the good MIGs—the planes your soldiers destroyed were waiting for repairs.'' While we were there, Amin would walk among the crowds and drive his jeep about town to show that he was not afraid of showing himself in public. Yet, he employed witch doctors and seers to instruct him in methods of warding off the evil spirits. We were also told that Amin did not dare come to New York for the UN session until President Mobutu of Zaïre had assured him that adequate security would be provided. He was deathly afraid of an assassination attempt since there were so many Ugandan exiles in the United States. It is reported that now Amin is constantly surrounded by Palestinian and Nubian bodyguards. For a while, he did not use the command post or the presidential residence in Entebbe, but instead, sequestered himself in the Nile Hotel, a multistoried modern building in the center of Kampala.

Amin's political ideology changed according to his chance for success. He was intensely loyal to the British during the Mau Mau uprising. He supported Obote's defeat of the monarchy of Buganda. He sought Baganda brains and approval when he seized power. He extolled Israelis when they gave him military equipment. He turned against Zionists and Jews when he became an Arab nationalist. He became an anti-imperialist in an effort to purge the Uganda economy of all foreign control. Then, he brought Palestinians, Arab, and Soviet technicians to aid the ailing economy.

There were areas of disagreement between the Communist Chinese diplomats and ourselves, but on one occasion, the Chinese ambassador remarked, ''Amin is a man without philosophy.'' Indeed, he is a man with no ideology. His former foreign minister and brother-in-law, Wanume Kibedi, remarked, ''Amin held the power but did not know what to do with it. He did not have any policies of any kind—political, economic, or social.''

As time passed, Amin became more and more entrenched. His fearlessness was really ruthlessness. He gave orders for thousands to be killed.

Amin still claimed his allegiance to the poor and desperate masses. ''The poorest man in Uganda is General Amin. It is better for me to be poor and the people richer.'' Western dip-

111

lomats, pressmen, and political leaders saw Amin's Economic War as a farce. The people were not getting richer—except for a handful of Amin's closest military officers. Instead, a reign of terror was taking place in which there seemed to be no end.

Third World leaders and political analysts did nothing. A few took delight in Amin's successful slaps at the Western powers. Most, however, retreated from the issue claiming that it was an internal matter. President Julius Nyerere of Tanzania was an exception. For he had supported the Obote claim from the beginning and even gave Obote a staging area for his attempted invasion. When Amin decided to expel the Asians, Nyerere called him a "racist." Kenneth Kaunda also denounced Amin, saying that he was a "madman."

Nigeria, Ghana, Sudan, Zäire, Rwanda, and Libya had embassies in Kampala. Many of the others handled Ugandan affairs from their embassies in Nairobi. A few of these African diplomats whom we had come to know very well privately spoke of their abhorrence and disapproval of Amin and his actions. Nevertheless, their governments took no specific action and made no comment on the growing tyranny present in Uganda.

In the summer of 1975, Uganda was finally scheduled to host the summit meeting of the Organization of African Unity. Each year, the meeting takes place at one of the African capitals on a rotation basis. The head of state who hosts the meeting is automatically chosen as chairman of the OAU and plays that role until the following yearly meeting. Under Obote, Uganda had completed construction of a magnificent conference center located in Kampala in anticipation of the OAU meeting. The coup took place and the meeting site was changed. Finally in 1975, Uganda, under Amin, was to have the coveted meeting.

Ordinarily, the OAU summit meeting is an important date for African heads of state. They have fully supported the young organization and normally attend the summit meeting each year. One of the main topics for the organization is the southern African question. The OAU has actively supported liberation groups in southern Africa through a special committee.

According to some reports there were maneuvers behind the

scenes to prevent Idi Amin from becoming chairman of the OAU. A plan was formulated to suggest that in honor of the monumental task that Mozambique liberation fighters had accomplished in bringing about independence for their country, Samora Machel, the president of Mozambique, should be given the chairmanship. The plan was, however, dropped when backers lacked sufficient support. Arab states were firmly behind Amin. Other governments continued to claim a hands-off attitude. In the end, African states had serious reservations about Amin's leadership of the OAU, but they were reluctant to cause any wide-scale dissension or division in the organization. Many felt that the southern African question and the continuance of white minority domination in those areas is the prime political issue for African states. To divert attention from this issue would be self-defeating. Some even believed that having Amin as spokesman might enhance the issue, for he certainly had the courage to be forthright in words and actions.

But one African group did publicly speak out against Amin. The Union of Writers of African Peoples, meeting in Accra in June 1975 passed a resolution calling on African heads of state to abandon Kampala as the venue of the next OAU summit. It furthermore called on African writers to disseminate the truth about the horrors in Uganda. Attached to a list of those dead, the union issued a statement expressing "its profound indignation against all attempts at the denial of human dignity, freedom and security, as is certainly the situation in Uganda and South Africa, not to mention the other concentration camps on the continent."

Wole Soyinka, the Nigerian playwright, has long been known for his forthright discussion and criticism of political trends and practices in his own country. As coordinating secretary of the union, he led the writers to take a firm stand on what he saw as "Amin's homicide."

Thus, as Africans gathered for the meeting in Kampala, delegates winced when asked by reporters about Amin becoming chairman. Just a week before, Amin had staged one of his farcical scenes. At a party in Kampala, Amin made his entrance in a sedan chair being carried by four European businessmen. This playful parody of the "white man's burden" drew both laughter

113

and embarrassment from the African officials assembling for the meeting.

Actually, the OAU meeting drew far fewer than the usual heads of state in attendance at such meetings. Presidents Nyerere and Kaunda refused to attend. Seretse Khama of Botswana also declined to go to Kampala for security reasons. The Mozambique president also was absent but sent a delegation to accept membership for the newly independent state. In fact, only nineteen of Africa's forty-six heads of state attended.

During the meeting, Amin performed a mock attack on Cape Town, South Africa, off an island in Lake Victoria. Amin had recently taken the new title Field Marshal to prepare to lead the battle in southern Africa. ''We are already raising an army,'' he said. ''When they start fighting, you are going to see a fire bigger than in Northern Ireland.'' It sounded ridiculous to Western observers, but to Africans the subject was serious, and not entirely far-fetched.

By the time Amin arrived in New York for the United Nations General Assembly meeting, on October 1, 1975, a number of African governments and their representatives still hoped that Amin's knack for gaining headline attention would be put to use for the southern African cause. Amin staged a magnificent show by his attack on Israel, but the issue of southern Africa was hardly even mentioned because of the preoccupation with Amin's ''anti-Zionist'' tirade. Daniel Moynihan, the U.S. ambassador to the United Nations, said in a speech, ''It's no accident, I fear, that this 'racist murderer'—as one of our leading newspapers called him this morning—is head of the Organization of African States.'' Moynihan's remarks caused a fury in United Nations halls. Many African delegates were incensed. The ambassador from Dahomey blasted Moynihan for ''a deliberately provocative act vis-à-vis President Amin and an unfriendly act toward the OAU.'' There was an attempt to rally African delegates to defend their organization's choice of chairman. The old argument of being wary of those who attempted to ''divide and rule'' was once again used to prevent African delegates from breaking ranks. Officially, most African governments lamented Moynihan's remarks. Yet, Moynihan had stirred the consciences of those who privately regretted their association with the tyrannical leader. A few mildly declared Moynihan had overreacted.

In another communication to President Ford, I had urged that the President correct the impression left by the fact that a member of the U.S. delegation present during Amin's speech at the UN did not walk out during the address. "We will be stronger people when we establish as a concrete policy our determination not to show any amenities to a tyrant who is murdering his own people and publicly endorsing genocide and extinction for another country."

A few days later, the President's press secretary, Ron Nessen, declared that the President fully supported Moynihan's use of the term "racist murderer" to describe Amin.

Some State Department members and other observers of African politics believed that Moynihan's remarks would only serve the cause of promoting Amin as an African hero.

In remarks at the United Nations, Amin also addressed American blacks. He claimed that American blacks had been barred from policy-making roles in the U.S. government because of divisions among themselves. Clarence Mitchell, Jr., an official of the National Association for the Advancement of Colored People who was serving as a U.S. delegate on the UN General Assembly, rejected Amin's "unsolicited advice on how black Americans should conduct their affairs." In an interview with the *Amsterdam News*, a leading black newspaper, Amin said he expressed his disappointment at not being invited to visit Harlem, for he wanted to see for himself the damages that the Zionist movement had done to Harlem and its people.

The bid for American black support had been initiated while we were still in Uganda. In early 1973, Amin sent a good-will mission to several European countries and the United States. Contacts were made with black journalists and other leaders in the black community. Amin misjudged black Americans' attitudes. Black Americans were becoming more involved in the efforts of African freedom-fighters in Zimbabwe (Rhodesia) and South Africa, where black Africans were suffering under white minority rule. Their increased interest and activity in African issues did not mean that they would support any African regime.

115

Blacks in the United States who endured second-class citizenship and numerous insults to their dignity were, by and large, not going to respond to the invitation of a tyrant.

A number of others have gone on record calling Amin a "capricious, brutal despot." Recently, black churchmen and women have come to the aid of exiled Ugandan prelates in their attempt to help those who have fled. A letter to the *New York Times* aptly stated the position of many black Americans on the subject. "We in the [American] black community long opposed the brutality, the oppression, and the injustices of the white minority governments of South Africa and Rhodesia. We are equally outraged by the violations of human rights and the murders committed by President Idi Amin Dada of Uganda. Neither the character nor the quality of oppression is altered when it is a black tyrant who is killing other blacks."

Amin actually tried to capitalize on his own racism. He attempted to woo black Americans by posing as a true black hero. Andrew Young, the first black U.S. Ambassador to the United Nations, whose blunt language on racial equality is well known, commented on Uganda and Amin. "Death in Uganda seems to be a matter of government policy on specific groups of people. It's like Hitler's pogrom of the Jews. . . . I want him [Amin] to disappear from the face of the earth." Young's statements came only a year and a half after Moynihan's criticism of Amin. There were no real objections to Young's remarks. People might argue that Young was black and acceptable to Third World delegates, and Amin is no longer chairman of the Organization of African Unity, the symbol of African solidarity. The real reason is that at last people are beginning to awaken to the fact that Amin is not just a comical character—but a cruel and ruthless tyrant who poses a threat to the African continent.

In June 1977, a conference of heads of governments from the Commonwealth countries met in London. The conference coincided with the Queen's celebration of her twenty-fifth anniversary as monarch. Great Britain, however, informed the Ugandan government that Idi Amin would not be welcome at the meeting nor at the Queen's jubilee celebration. Amin, however, threatened to arrive in London. He circulated a story that he would fly to Europe and reach England by boat. The Ugandan government even announced that the three hundred Britons residing in Uganda would not be permitted to leave until Amin returned from London to decide their fate. The British government ignored these threats and claimed that Amin was just trying to steal the headlines away from the Commonwealth meeting.

Anti-Amin feelings had grown considerably in London and among the visiting Commonwealth delegations. Shortly before the meeting opened, the *Sunday Times* (London) printed a long interview given by the defecting Minister Kyemba, who implicated Amin in the death of the Anglican archbishop as well as Mrs. Dora Bloch, one of the Israeli passengers aboard the hijacked Air France plane.

Kenneth Kaunda, president of Zambia, gave a television interview in which he, too, compared Amin to Hitler and called him an "essentially evil man." Prime Minister Michael Manley of Jamaica, who has been taking an increasingly active role in Third World affairs, said that Amin was "a cause of shame for all mankind." He accused Third World leaders of a double standard for condemning "racist tyranny" in white ruled southern Africa while ignoring Amin. Manley said, "We should not hesitate, therefore, to denounce tyranny, whether of the tribal, military, or fascist kind when it is found in our own ranks." By the end of the week, Amin had not appeared in London, and in fact, he never left Uganda.

At the close of their meeting in June 1977, the Commonwealth heads of government condemned Amin's regime in Uganda for its "disregard for the sanctity of human life" and its "massive violation of basic human rights." The excesses in Uganda were "so gross as to warrant the world's concern and to evoke condemnation by heads of government in strong and unequivocal terms." In order for the leaders to come to some agreement on the communique, some compromises were made. Amin's name was omitted in the document that spoke of an "overwhelming view" rather than unanimous opinion of the participants. Despite the concessions, this was the first time a group of heads of government issued a public attack on Amin's government.

117

While we were in Uganda in 1972–1973, it was popular in some groups to refer to Amin as an African folk hero. Within a few weeks of our arrival there, we came to the firm conclusion that he was a shrewd tyrant. Later when we returned to the U.S.A., it would pain us to hear the word hero used to describe Amin in 1974, 1975, 1976, and 1977.

7: THE SECOND PERSECUTION

A TRIBAL CHIEF, ABOUT FIFTY YEARS OLD, A CHRISTIAN, AND AN exemplary father and husband, was arrested early one morning. He was condemned to death that afternoon. His legs and arms were cut off and he was left in agony; he died three days later.

Another man, a military officer and chaplain, similarly was arrested and taken to prison. He was locked in a cell with thirty-seven other men, some of whom were crying out in pain because their legs or arms had been broken. He died the next day of twenty-two gunshot and stab wounds.

These two gruesome incidents were about eighty-five years apart. The first was a martyr in the terrible persecution of Ugandan Christians which took place under the Kabaka Mwanga, the king of Buganda between 1885 and 1887. The second was a victim of the present persecution of Christians being waged under Idi Amin in Uganda.

In October 1964, Margaret flew to Rome to attend the canonization ceremony which elevated twenty-two martyrs of the first Christian persecution to sainthood. She recalls the brilliance of the historic event. St. Peter's was filled with color—races of all shades, flowing robes of bright hues contrasting with the sedate black veils of the European diplomatic corps. The marble walls of the ancient church resounded with the free-throated singing of a male and female Ugandan choir. It was the first time that women's voices were heard for a Pontifical Mass in St. Peter's. Drums beat, the wooden African xylophone rang. Pope Paul VI entered the great central door behind a huge standard of the Ugandan martyrs. Assisting the Pope at mass was the late Archbishop Joseph Kiwanuka, who had served twenty-five years as bishop in Uganda. Slowly and dramatically the Holy Father entoned twenty-two new names—African names like Mukasa, Kizito, and Lwanga, inscribing them into the Holy Catalog of Saints. Margaret was seated among Ugandan friends. She remembered seeing the joy and excitement on the faces of the Ugandan laymen and women so heavily committed to the work of their local church parishes.

Some of those same faces are no longer present, for they met their death during the second Christian persecution under Idi Amin.

In 1969, Pope Paul VI visited Uganda to make a pilgrimage to the site where the martyrs had been burned. It was the first time a Pope had touched African soil. Our Ugandan friends told us of how they set out during the night to take up positions at the shrine about 3 A.M. Thousands of Ugandans waited there until noon, when the Holy Father arrived.

It was natural for the Holy Father to choose Uganda as the one African country he would visit. We remember passing a simple brick fireplace-like monument on the shores of Lake Victoria near Entebbe. The inscription read, "On this spot landed the first Catholic missionaries of Uganda on the 17th day of February in the Year of Our Lord 1879." The two missionaries were of the order of the White Fathers. They had traveled from an Indian Ocean port in Tanzania through the interior to Lake Victoria and then crossed the lake to the Northern shore in a dug-out canoe. When they arrived at the court of the Buganda ruler Mutesa, they were imprisoned. Mutesa was wary of the strangers. He had permitted English Protestant missionaries to enter his kingdom the preceding year. Though these men spoke a different European tongue—French—still they preached of another Church of God. After days of imprisonment, the men were led into the magnificent bamboo and grass palace of the *kabaka*. Mutesa's court was assembled. All were dressed elegantly for the occasion. The *kabaka*, Mutesa, stretched on his couch, questioned them before deciding to allow them to stay.

Thereafter, both Protestant and Catholic missionaries labored in Buganda. They both held services at court and competed for the *kabaka*'s attention. The constant feuding between the two Christian groups confused the ruler, who understood only that they were from two different and competing European powers. Nevertheless, both Protestant and Catholic groups succeeded in converting and baptizing among the people of the Buganda kingdom. The Moslems, too, were making inroads in Uganda. Once when confronted with the competing religions, the *kabaka* had decreed, "Let every man pray as he wishes." Later in his reign, enemies of the court forced the Catholic priests to leave. However, there was already a small but strong community of Catholics—Andrew Kaggwa, director of the king's bank; Joseph Mukasa, personal servant to the king; Mathias Murumba, a sub-chief; Matthew Kisule, the king's gunsmith; Charles Lwanga, the country's outstanding athlete and hero. Then Catholics went underground visiting the priests across the lake from time to time to receive the sacraments.

When Mutesa died, his son Mwanga acceded to the throne. A cruel and chaotic reign began. Wives who ceased to please the *kabaka* or pages who responded too slowly were mutilated and left to slowly die. Mwanga seemed to delight in watching someone die slowly. The king's rage turned on the Christians. He ordered the death of the newly appointed Anglican bishop James Hannington. Then he purged both Catholic and Protestants from his court, ordering them to be executed. Mwanga gave them one chance to deny their faith, but all refused. Andrew Kaggwa was decapitated. Pontain Ngondwe was stabbed by lances. Mathias Kalemba had his arms cut off at the elbows and his legs at the knees. Arteries and veins were tied so that he would not die too quickly. Bits of flesh were sliced from his body and roasted before his eyes.

A hundred people died that day because they were Christians, or suspected of being Christian. The young boys who worked as pages at the court were tied together and marched to the execution place in Namugongo, about sixteen miles from the *kabaka*'s palace. The executioner lit the reeds with a torch. As the flames consumed the martyrs, they prayed aloud to the God of their Christian faith.

These terrible persecutions left a martyr tradition to the Catholic and Protestant churches in Uganda that is unmatched in other parts of Africa. Despite the early setbacks, the trials of Ugandan Christians seemed to be a strengthening factor, for the Christian community grew quickly and extensively.

In the years that we have known and visited Africa, we have heard many and varied views of the role of the Christian missionaries in Africa. They came not only as the messengers of Christ but as teachers and doctors. They were the first to build and maintain schools and hospitals for the African people. In the early period, if a person could read he was automatically assumed to be Christian, for only at the mission could the people learn to read and write. The missionaries brought medicines and taught the people simple lessons of hygiene. Throughout the continent we have been impressed with the sacrifice and dedication of the missionaries of all denominations. We remember speaking to a Moslem head of state who told us of his disappointment with technical assistance programs from various Eastern and Western nations. "They spend much of their time insisting on comfortable housing and air conditioning. On the other hand, the missionaries come to stay, bearing many hardships and living with the people. Those sent by their governments will not deal with the most difficult problems. They will not care for the lepers. Only the Christian missionaries would spend their lives doing that." Another Christian leader, when he visited Washington, explained that he had to decline the offer of the Peace Corps but instead suggested that the U.S. government find ways to finance the worthy projects of missionaries. "The missionaries do not come for just two years, they stay a lifetime. These long-term efforts are worth so much more in developing the country."

Some Africans bitterly lament the missionaries' cooperation with the colonial powers. In Uganda, the Christian missions encouraged the British to bring peace to a land rocked by the chaotic actions of the *kabakas*. They encouraged British "protection." Furthermore, some Africans lament the Westernization of the people by the missionaries. Marriage and sexual customs were changed whereby tribal ceremonies and traditions were discarded for Christian puritanical codes. Even the official dress of women in Buganda, the Busuti, is a Westernized form of dress which the Christian missionaries sought to place on the scantily clothed Ugandan women. Some forms of dances and other rituals thought to be too pagan for the early Christians were suppressed.

The Christian missionaries built schools and hospitals, but they were also criticized for not Africanizing fast enough. However, in Uganda a special effort was made to form African priests in both the Anglican and Catholic churches. The first two priests from Buganda were ordained in 1913—a mere two generations before the black African bishop, Joseph Kiwanuka, who was ordained by Pope Pius XII in the late 1930s.

A shameful aspect of the Christianization of Uganda was the complete division between the Protestant and Catholic missions. The intense rivalry and suspicion was transmitted to the African population. These frictions developed into open fighting in 1892. The colonial administration then divided the country into zones where Catholics and Anglicans were to exercise their work separately and without competition. In Buganda, the Catholics centered their activity in Masaka just south of Entebbe.

The divisions continued, and despite a modern era of ecumenism, distinctions are still made. In the immediate period preceding independence even the two political parties were split along religious lines. Benedicto Kiwanuka and his Democratic party were considered the Catholic faction, while Obote and his party were considered Protestant.

We had expected to find a thriving Christian community in Uganda. There had been initial concern about the fact that Idi Amin was a Moslem ruling a predominantly Christian country; but from his statements at the time, there had been no cause for alarm. Amin began his regime by attempting to fuse unity throughout the country and urged religious cooperation among all groups. In fact, he saw himself as the instrument of that unity of faith. He carefully chose to be present at various religious functions. First the Anglican cathedral, then the Moslem mosque, then the Catholic cathedral would be visited by him and his entourage. He established a Department of Religious Affairs within the government and called a conference of religious leaders. At first many believed that Amin was truly interested in breaking down some of the barriers that had existed between various religious groups. Many initially cooperated, for they saw Amin's interest as an important ecumenical step.

From the very beginning, Amin portrayed himself as a religious man. A few days after the successful coup, Amin invited fifty religious leaders to meet with him. He assured them, "Whatever I do will be done for God and my country." He urged the people to live cleanly and follow their respective religions. God was often mentioned in his speech. At first, he gave the impression to everyone that he was a man of faith. He feared no one but God. Later, he led the people to believe that he was not only a faithful follower of God but a prophet. When he announced his decree regarding the expulsion of the Asians, he told the people that he had been led by God in a dream to take these actions against the Asian aliens. In one of his later tirades against the Zionists, he attempted to stir Christian hatred against the Jews by intimating Jewish responsibility for the death of Christ.

As we watched Amin's relationships grow with the Arab states, we noticed how he used his Moslem religious affiliation to spur a feeling of solidarity. We were told that Amin deliberately exaggerated the Moslem percentage of the Ugandan population in order to please his new friends.

Amin was able to raise funds from Arab states to support mosques and Islamic activities. We learned that on the occasion of the visit of Libyan President Colonel Qaddafi to Uganda, Qaddafi addressed a crowd at the University of Makerere. Having been misled by Amin's inflated picture of the Islamic composition of Uganda, the Libyan president began attacking Israel and Christianity. During his passionate speech on Islam, the students and professors quietly walked out in silent protest. It became apparent that Amin was shrewdly displaying a religiosity to insure that the people would not only respect his decisions, but fear his wrath. Furthermore, he used the power of God to carry on his wars—those against the Zionists, and the Asians—as well as his effort to solidify a convenient friendship with the Arab states.

It first became clear to the people that a purge of Christians was taking place in September 1972, soon after we arrived. The civilians who were killed or who "disappeared" after the attempted invasion were largely prominent figures in the Christian community. Benedicto Kiwanuka, the first prime minister of Uganda, was a leading Catholic political figure. Joseph Mubiru also was an active Catholic. The former mayor of Masaka, who had been knighted by the Pope, was dragged in front of the crowd of people, stripped and bound. He begged to speak by telephone to Amin. The chief killer took a knife, cut off his penis, and held it before the face of the screaming man. "Use this to telephone Kampala," the soldier said. And he threw his victim into a waiting vehicle. Neither Catholic priests nor Protestant pastors were immune from Amin's killer squad. A Ugandan pastor was accused of treason for having read on a radio church broadcast the Old Testament prophecy of Israel's future triumph over its enemies. He was charged with supporting the Zionist cause. He was murdered.

In August 1972, the Catholic Episcopal Conference of Africa and Madagascar took place in Uganda. Amin attended the opening of the conference, which was at Gaba Institute in Kampala, a well-known pastoral training center for African priests and laity. During the conference, Amin invited the visiting Catholic cardinals and bishops to a state dinner at which he drank a toast to the "future peace and welfare of the Catholic Church." One of the church dignitaries chose not to attend the state dinner. He privately told me that he would not eat with a man who had recently embarked on a racist plan to eliminate all Asians from Uganda.

The Catholic church in Uganda had not endorsed Amin's first phase of the Economic War—that of expelling the Asians. As a result, Amin was furious with the Catholic archbishop, Emmanual Nsubuga. In December 1972, he accused the Catholic prelate of being in league with the "Zionists and South African imperialists" and placed him under surveillance. Amin had a letter published which supposedly implicated the Archbishop in plans to overthrow the government. During the heated argument, Nsubuga was quietly called to Rome and then returned after the situation had cooled down.

In the meantime, at the end of 1972 Margaret became a member of the parish council of one of the Catholic churches in Kampala. It was an experience that she will never forget. She likened the atmosphere to that of the early church in Rome. On Sundays, the church was filled to capacity with people lined up on the steps trying to squeeze their way inside. Those who previously had been lax in church attendance had suddenly returned. The parish community became closely knit helping each other in their moments of trial. African members of the council became particularly concerned with the future fate of the church. They began planning for every eventuality, painstakingly working out financial and administrative details in case the leadership, and especially the priests of the church, were suddenly eliminated by Amin's henchmen. There was a martyr mystique in the parish. Many seemed to wait in expectation of arrest. Margaret remembers vividly that some of the men would remark that they had made all provisions at home and within the church administration in preparation for their imminent death. They went about their work calmly, but with a tremendous and fervent faith. The twenty-two martyrs of Uganda were indeed an inspiration to them now as they faced Amin's reign of terror.

Amin had set out to become the unifying force in the religious community of Uganda. Unity to Amin meant following him without question, but church leaders were not prepared to endorse his cruel and murderous methods. Amin quickly learned that the churches would not submit easily to his schemes.

Amin used several methods to intimidate the churches. At various times, he would warn the churches against preaching false doctrines. From time to time soldiers would arrive at missions and search the premises. Missionary sisters and priests who used to be able to travel freely and easily in Uganda were suddenly subject to scrutiny and questioning. They would often be stopped and harassed at roadblocks.

In October, 1972, I had already arranged for the departure of American Jewish citizens, Peace Corps volunteers, and wives and dependents who wished to leave. The embassy was also completing most contracts with private Americans. There remained, however, besides the official representation of Embassy and AID personnel, about five hundred private Americans. They were mostly missionaries. We ordered the embassy staff to update and verify all information on U.S. citizens in Uganda. If there was ever a serious immediate threat to security, we had to be able to communicate quickly with all these Americans. We had a clear and heavy responsibility to inform these Americans of the danger they faced. Therefore, I asked to return to Washington on consultation to discuss with Secretary of State William Rogers and Assistant Secretary of State David Newsom the growing security situation and to present my ideas on the reduction of Americans present in Uganda. When I returned in November to Kampala, I had a clear plan to execute. The private

Americans—mostly missionaries—were scattered throughout Uganda. We had to travel to various points in the interior and meet with representatives of as many of the mission groups as possible.

After the deadline for the departure of Asians had passed, we used the lull in activity to travel outside of the Kampala area. We sent messages ahead asking missionaries to plan small gatherings so we could meet with them. In each case, I cautioned them not to involve everyone, for the presence of large numbers could possibly make Ugandan soldiers suspicious of our purpose.

In a sense, we were pleased to have the opportunity of traveling, for we had not had any chance to see the more remote areas of Uganda. We knew though that, despite our diplomatic car and its U.S. flag, we were not protected from the changing temper and mood of the Uganda army. In every case, we would inform the Uganda government through the foreign office of our intended itinerary—but since we knew that the foreign office had little leverage with the military, the information supplied would hardly guarantee our security.

By this time, few dared travel the roads. Most of the Asian community had left. Uganda was still closed to tourists. On one trip we had to pass by the Queen Elizabeth Game Park. When we arrived late in the evening at the hotel, the Ugandan manager was waiting at the door to greet us. "Where were you?" he asked. "We have been waiting all day for you." They had not had any guests in a fortnight. Most of the staff had been let go, and those who remained were ecstatic to see guests arrive. They fell all over us to provide service, though the menu was limited. We had about four waiters at our side during the entire meal. The manager of the hotel was equally distraught when we told him we were staying only one night for we were on our way to another town. The next morning, as we ate breakfast, we looked out at the vast plains that reached towards the Zaïre border. Several years ago, we had approached these same plains and mountains from the park in Eastern Zaïre. The area was rich in magnificent game, peacefully following nature's cycles as they had done for hundreds of generations. The vast herds of zoological specimens in these same glorious and natural settings had drawn many

127

people to Uganda, including Theodore Roosevelt in the early part of this century. Now there was no big game hunting, just watching and photographing. This was truly a precious resource to preserve and show the world. As we left the park behind, we wondered if we would ever have the opportunity of seeing it again. If, already, human life in Uganda had lost its value, then what chance had the herds of buffalo and gazelle. Soldiers thought nothing of killing off a buffalo for meat or poaching on elephants to extract the still valuable ivory tusks.

We met with both Catholic and Protestant groups throughout the country. I discussed frankly the security situation with them. Repeatedly I stressed that the U.S. Embassy might not be able to guarantee their safety in the country. I urged them to think carefully before deciding to remain in Uganda. A number of missionaries, particularly those who had families, had decided to leave. Others who gradually saw their mission eroding, either from various restrictions or fear on the part of the Ugandan community, began to make plans to withdraw. For the younger members, it was not easy to work under the duress and pressure always present. They were constantly under surveillance, sometimes by people working within their own mission. Some began to feel that their presence, as Americans in the Ugandan community, was actually harmful for the Ugandan Christians who were often threatened because of their association with foreigners.

The Pastoral Institute at Gaba was a regional center for Catholic priests and laity who came to spend one year of intensive study in an in-service program designed to update a person's theological background and acquaint him with new trends and methods. It was a meeting place for Catholics from many different countries in East and Central Africa. As soon as the troubles between Tanzania and Uganda increased, Tanzanian trainees were refused entrance into Uganda. Furthermore, tales of killings and disappearances spread throughout Africa, and applicants for the program declined. No one wanted to come to Uganda. The institute also depended on a free atmosphere of exchange. Soon it became impossible to function since every word or comment had to be carefully formed so as not to risk being accused of subversion. The institute finally closed and moved to another nearby African country.

A number of American missionaries had worked in Uganda for many long years. They were committed to the people. Since their lives had been largely spent in Uganda, they did not see any purpose in leaving. These missionaries were prepared to die. The older church men and women had urged us not to waste our time in trying to convince them of the dangers of remaining in Uganda. They had not come here in association with the U.S. government, but as members of their respective churches. They did not look to the U.S. government for help, and never would.

When I returned to Washington at the end of February, I contacted the U.S. headquarters of 15 Catholic and Protestant missionary groups with personnel in Uganda. I counseled them to be careful about written communication and briefed them on the security situation. Most appreciated the advice and agreed not to send any new personnel for the time being. Furthermore, many decided to make reductions where possible.

In the end, when the U.S. Embassy was withdrawn in the fall of 1973, only about 240 Americans remained. They were, and still are, mostly missionaries. I believed that I and other U.S. government officials had spoken clearly and plainly to those who chose to stay. Without the embassy they could not expect rescue or assistance if they were threatened or arrested.

Such a situation surfaced in February 1977, when Amin became angered over condemnations coming from the U.S. He insisted on detaining all Americans for a meeting. I was in contact with the White House on possible reactions of the U.S. government. It was President Carter's first foreign crisis. The President decided to act with strength and decision. He sent a message warning Amin that the U.S. government would not tolerate any attempt to hold Americans hostage.

In a few days, the crisis ended with Amin postponing indefinitely the American meeting and lifting all travel restrictions. During those few days, however, Amin had kept the international press busy with additional remarks, threats, and insinuations regarding the fate of the two hundred Americans. In the end, it was another cover-up. Refugees poured across the border into Kenya telling horrible stories of yet another bloodbath. As the world watched and worried over the fate of a group of Americans, mostly missionaries dedicated to promulgating the Christian message of love and justice, Amin was slaughtering large numbers of his own people.

Amin next attempted to threaten Great Britain with essentially the same action. When he was barred from attending the Commonwealth meeting in June 1977, he prohibited all Britons in Uganda from leaving until he had returned from his bid to enter the British Isles for the conference. James Callaghan, the British prime minister, remained calm during these developments, saying that it was one of Amin's many bluffs. In an interview, Callaghan remarked that the three hundred Britons knew when they decided to stay what might befall them. The Commonwealth, he said, "must set out what it feels on certain issues."

The presence of Americans in a foreign country has always complicated our foreign relations. It is easy to say that the U.S. must speak out and criticize wherever it observes gross violations against human rights. Certainly in Uganda, where an intolerable tyrant exists, there is no question of our position. At the same time, it would be equally difficult for us to stand still and see our U.S. citizens threatened or held as hostages.

When Amin had expelled fifty-five Catholic missionaries, at the end of 1972, we began to think that Amin would attempt to rid Uganda of missionaries as he had done with the Asians. The missionaries had been charged with being mercenaries in disguise who had hidden arms and military uniforms beneath their robes. Among the group expelled was a ninety-year-old missionary who had spent sixty years in Uganda—hardly a person to be feared by Idi Amin! When the Ugandan Catholic Archbishop Nsubuga protested to the President, Amin turned his wrath against the prelate, "You must pray to God for forgiveness."

By that time, a delegation had been sent by Paul VI to review the presence of missionaries in Uganda. The Vatican was alarmed by the expulsion of the fifty-five and was hoping to avoid any further action by Amin. When the delegation met with Amin, he told them that his actions were led by God and that the Defense Council had advised him that Uganda must rely more on its own resources—even in religious matters. Nevertheless, he claimed that the missionaries were welcome in Uganda and that he planned to visit the Holy Father on his next trip to Europe. In

1975, Amin did visit the Vatican and had an audience with Pope Paul VI. But the papal delegation and the Vatican visit failed, as had other leaders and groups. Even the Pope had found it impossible to reason with such a tyrant.

In January 1973, the editor of the Catholic newspaper *Munno* was found murdered in his burned-out car. *Munno* had been established in 1911. It was at the time the only Catholic daily newspaper in Africa. Two other black Ugandan editors, Samuel Mwebe and John Serwaniko, were also killed. By 1976, Amin had tired of trying to silence the newspaper by eliminating editors. He had the paper disbanded and closed.

Later that year, soldiers entered a church in Masaka. Father Clement Musoke was celebrating mass. The soldiers went to the altar and dragged the priest away. His torn vestments were later found beside the road; the priest was never seen again. At the time, Father Musoke had been known as an outspoken priest.

Amin would frequently claim, "We do not believe in propaganda, but in truth. We speak the truth." But Ugandans had no longer any faith in their government sources of information. They instead turned to their churches, not only to be comforted, but to seek accurate and straight information. They were tired of listening to insipid statements, and instead had crowded the churches to hear priests and pastors like Father Musoke.

There seemed to be no end in sight. The murders, disappearances, and tortures continued. Finally in August of 1976, the church decided that it could not continue to remain passive. A meeting was called of all Ugandan religious leaders. With a representative from the Moslem Council present, they searched for ways of tempering the regime. The group decided to concentrate on the excessive and extreme punishments for insignificant and minor crimes. They drew up some resolutions to be presented to President Amin suggesting that the death sentence was too extreme for crimes such as overcharging.

Amin, however, was in no mood to accept recommendations from the religious leaders. He was shrewd enough to realize that the Christian churches would not be easily silenced. They were too independent. They had too many ties to the outside world

131

through their missionaries and their international organizations. Reports of new purges, of bodies mutilated and floating in the Nile River, of trucks coming from the prisons loaded with dead bodies, often filtered out through church members. Amin believed that the Anglican archbishop, Janani Luwum, had inspired the religious leaders' meeting in August. He decided to break the power of the church and begin at the very top. He had succeeded in destroying the power of other groups through the same methods. At Christmas, 1976, Amin made the accusation that "some bishops were preaching bloodshed."

Early in the morning on February 5, 1977, Ugandan soldiers entered the compound of the Archbishop Luwum. Tricking the prelate into opening the door, they began searching his house. With a gun thrust in his side, they searched the Archbishop from head to foot. Repeatedly, they shouted, "Show us the arms." They looked everywhere—in the food storage bins, the chapel, and bathrooms—for the cache of ammunition and guns which the Archbishop supposedly had hidden. Nothing was found. That same evening Bishop Yona Okoth, the Anglican bishop of Bukedi was also searched.

The church leaders decided that they could not sit back silently. The Archbishop and other Anglican bishops met on February 8. They drafted a letter to Amin, bitterly complaining about being searched and accused by soldiers. Further, they dared to enumerate some of the serious matters that concerned the entire Christian community. The letter declared that the security of Christians was in jeopardy. "We have buried many who have died as a result of being shot and there are many more whose bodies have not been found." They accused Amin of favoring the Moslems over other religious communities and spoke of "a war against the educated which is forcing many of our people to run away." The fear and instability were cited: "The gun which was meant to protect Uganda as a nation is increasingly being used against the Ugandan to take away his life and his property." And lastly, they identified the State Research Bureau as a body whose members "arrest and kill at will innocent individuals." Never before had a group or individual dared to voice these same concerns from within Uganda. Amin was stunned. He had thought that the searching of the prelates' houses would shake them with fright; not provoke a fight!

At midnight on Sunday, February 13, Amin telephoned the Archbishop and scolded him with abuse. He summoned the prelate to Entebbe the following day. Amin had been incensed over a report in a London newspaper that a wave of killings was underway in Uganda and that the Archbishop had been arrested. Photos were taken of Luwum and Amin together to prove to the foreign press that the Archbishop was very much alive.

An English army officer, once Amin's commander, had tea with the Archbishop that same afternoon at the State House. He chatted with the Archbishop and his wife, who seemed relaxed and unaware of the gravity of the situation. It was to be the lull before the storm.

The same day Amin accused the prelate of being implicated in a new attempt by Obote to overthrow the Uganda government. He charged that arms had been found on the Archbishop's property. The accusations and claims by Amin were broadcast that evening on radio and television news reports. As usual, nothing was mentioned about the Archbishop's categorical denial.

Archbishop Luwum and the other Anglican bishops prepared written rebuttals of the accusations but it was no use. Archbishop Luwum and two government ministers, Lieutenant Colonel Erinayo Oryema and Charles Oboth-Ofumbi, were brought before a crowd of three thousand soldiers. Details of the plot and accusations against the three men were read before the soldiers, onlooking diplomats, and government ministers. The Archbishop, dressed in his purple robes, shook his head at the accusations, but the crowd shouted, "Kill them, kill them now." The men were then put into a vehicle and driven away.

The next morning, Radio Uganda announced that the three men were dead after being involved in an automobile accident. Headlines cried, "Murder!" The Ugandan government announced that the bodies had already been buried. Memorial services were cancelled. Vatican Radio called it, "unswallowable," and termed the Archbishop a martyr. The world was indeed outraged. Shortly after Amin's press claimed that the Archbishop was killed in a car crash, I publicly called for a full UN investigation

Anglican Archbishop of Uganda, Janani Luwum, was reported killed in an automobile wreck in February 1977. A Ugandan minister later revealed that Luwum was murdered.

Nicholas Stroh, journalist, killed in Uganda in 1971, though circumstances of his death were never disclosed.

of the "car accident." President Carter later remarked at a news conference that "recent events in Uganda disgusted the entire civilized world." It was these comments and others by U.S. officials that sent Amin storming to retaliate by prohibiting American residents in Uganda from leaving.

The deaths were described by Henry Kyemba, Amin's minister of health, who defected in June 1977. In his statement from London, Kyemba said, "When an army lorry brought the bullet riddled bodies of Archbishop Luwum and the two Ministers to the mortuary, they were simply thrown out of the back of the truck like sacks of coffee. It was dreadful. The Archbishop was still in his robes, with a cross on a chain around his neck—in fact, all three were in the same clothes that they were wearing when they all attended an official arms demonstration earlier that day. And they had been shot at very close range several times."

Kyemba's story seemed to erase any doubts that the Archbishop of the Anglican church had been deliberately murdered.

In the aftermath, many of the Anglican bishops and churchmen had fled. They knew that they would be next. Some have told us about the risks that Christians take in Uganda. "When you say you are going to stand up as a Christian," one bishop said, "you had better count the price. It can cost you your head."

We visited the shrine of the martyrs at Namugongo outside of Kampala before leaving Uganda. A new church had been designed for this site using the conical lines of the traditional palaces of the Baganda *kabakas*. A fund had been started to help pay for its construction. As we flipped through the pages of the promotional literature on the new shrine, and looked at the peaceful site set in the hills of the lush countryside, we wondered how many more shrines would be needed to honor the present-day martyrs of Uganda.

The twenty-two martyrs proclaimed to be saints by Pope Paul VI met their death at the hands of a despotic and erratic ruler who was plagued by doubts, court enemies, and pagan loyalties. The martyrs of the twentieth century in Uganda also have been the victims of the rage of despotic rule, consumed by insecurity, fanaticism, and witchcraft. Recently, a Ugandan friend told us

135

that he truly believed the reports that Amin ate human livers, for his current witchdoctor had prescribed this horrible food to ward off evil spirits.

Perhaps this is an exaggerated tale; but the real facts of Amin's terror are proof enough of his evil and sinister ways. Despite the massacres, the churches are still filled. One churchman explained this phenomenon as an indication that the people of Uganda, being totally insecure physically, are searching at least for spiritual security.

A Ugandan Christian bidding farewell to friends a few years ago as he returned to Uganda said, ''We Christians in Uganda are ready to die for the Faith. Pray for us, please, that we will bravely face the ordeal.''

8: AN AMERICAN FAMILY IN UGANDA: ABROAD AND DIVIDED

ON FEBRUARY 8, 1973, I RECEIVED WORD FROM THE STATE Department to return immediately to Washington. If I wished, my family could be issued travel orders to depart Kampala with me. A quick decision had to be made. We had talked before about Margaret and the girls leaving, but we had not wished to be separated. If my consultation in Washington was to be only for a short time, then it would be foolish for the entire family to leave. Once dependents left areas threatened by insecure conditions, it was rare that the State Department permitted their return. We had to gamble on whether I would be returning or not. Margaret decided to stay.

For the next two months, while I worked in Washington, we saw Uganda from two different vantage points. Margaret, along with our daughters, was isolated; it was a time we will not soon forget. What follows is her account of these tumultuous months.

On the morning of February 8, I was playing golf on a course in a valley at the edge of the leading commercial hillside of Kampala. It had been a thriving colonial center of recreational and social activity for the British colonials, but now it was nearly empty. The Asians had left, the numbers of British and other European nationals had thinned, and African Ugandans had not expressed much interest in the sport. As with most athletic activity in the tropics, one had to play either in early morning or in the evening hours to avoid the dangers of sunstroke. I found it convenient from time to time to meet some other American or diplomatic women for a few hours of golf. It was relaxing because we could talk without fear of being overheard or taped.

We almost never talked of Ugandan politics at home unless we spoke in guarded or symbolic language. One had to assume that someone on the residence staff was being paid to report on everything he heard and saw at the U.S. Ambassador's home. This made life for families particularly difficult. During the first few months of our stay at our previous post, Burundi, I became somewhat depressed because it was such a complete change for me. Previously, Tom had always kept me informed of his activities. We had worked closely on many projects and in private life; we had traveled and interviewed many African heads of state and government officials together. I assisted Tom in the preparation of all of his books with the exception of his first two.

This could not be so in the diplomatic corps. Confidential, secret, and "Eyes only" memos were composed and carefully guarded in a small part of the embassy office. I had, therefore, to rely on Tom's briefing me on matters—but we could not be entirely candid at home. In Uganda, this situation was aggravated by the fact we kept a low profile in Uganda and we had little public contact with Ugandans outside of government officials. I made it a point, therefore, to visit the embassy office daily so that I could keep informed of at least a few of the developments.

When I walked up and down the many little hills of the golf course, my mind sometimes wandered. I imagined what might happen if suddenly there was an invasion or coup, and fighting broke out in the city. The open fairway of a golf course was hardly a place to take cover. On the morning of February 8, I saw one of the American embassy officials running across the course toward me. It was an emergency—but what kind of emergency——family, political, or security? I hurried to the embassy office with him. Tom told me about his orders to return to Washington for consultations at the Department of State. I thought for only a few moments and answered that I would stay. It was a gamble. I could always follow him out later.

Tom had less than a day to pack and clear his papers. In the midst of his preparations, he suddenly asked a photographer to come to take a picture of the entire family. Although we did not know it then, we would not be together for more than two months. Our daughters, then four and six, knew only that their Daddy was going back to Washington for a while. We had kept them shielded from events in Uganda. We did not want to frighten them and attempted to carry on a routine life for them. For security reasons, either I or our trusted housekeeper would accompany them to and from school in a chauffeur-driven car. They attended an international school staffed by Americans. The school itself had developed very rapidly over the years, but in the last few months it had experienced a drastic drop in its enrollment. There was an aura of uncertainty among the staff and administrators of the school, because they did not know how long they would be able to keep the school open. They were also concerned about the unsafe conditions. Plans had been formulated in case of an emergency, but they knew that these were useless, for the two homes which housed the school hardly gave any protection. The location was far from the embassy or American residences. If fighting broke out separating one part of the city from the others, it would be impossible to guarantee transportation home for the children. Knowing all these possibilities, they still continued to provide an education and hoped there would be no danger. Throughout the Asian expulsion, the invasion attempt in September, and the disappearances, the school functioned, hardly losing a day of classes.

But one day during school our oldest child, Tina, was told by a schoolmate that the American Ambassador had been kidnapped. Tina went into shock. Hearing "ambassador," she thought it was her father and she sobbed hysterically. When the teacher finally pieced the story together, she explained to Tina that indeed an American ambassador had been kidnapped and killed—but in Sudan. She returned home not entirely convinced and only a phone call to Washington assured her that her father was still alive and well.

The horrible murder of an American ambassador Hon. Cleo Allen and his deputy George C. Moore had indeed been close. Sudan was the northern neighbor of Uganda. The perpetrators were extremist Palestinians. We knew at the time that Palestinians were living and working in Kampala. While Tom was in Washington, his deputy, Robert Keeley, had appraised the situation as being so precarious that he ordered extra security measures. I remember that a special State Department team came to check all outside facilities. They ordered more grating, locks and heavy doors for one wing of our house. In addition, local Uganda police were assigned to guard our residence on a twenty-four-hour basis. Sometimes these policemen would sit in a leisurely way at our front door with rifle balanced against the back of the chair. I was continually afraid that one of the children might be lured into playing with the gun or accidentally set it off. The policemen were generally friendly and courteous. At night, however, they would sometimes appear overzealous. In the early morning hours, I would sometimes be awakened by the heavy clop of boots and the rattling of an outside door. Frightened at first, I soon discovered that about that time every night, the policeman would routinely check the outside of the house making sure that all doors were locked.

I was only able to sleep a few hours each night the entire time that I spent alone in Uganda. Sometimes I would wake to hear sporadic gunfire across the hillsides of the city. Occasionally I would hear the movement of trucks in the odd hours of the night.

We had installed radio communications between the embassy officers and the Marine guards at the embassy. After the Palestinian attack in Sudan, special precautions were taken at large social functions given at the embassy residences. For one lawn party given at our home, Marine guards were armed but dressed in civilian clothes. One was stationed on an upper-floor balcony with a rifle during the entire event.

It was not a pleasant way to live. We all tried to be sensible and cautious without overreacting, but at times this was impossible. I remember one night I had attended a film showing with our chargé d'affaires, Mr. Keeley and his wife. As we walked out to the car, I noticed two men who appeared to be Palestinians. They proceeded to a car nearby which was the same color and style as Mr. Keeley's. I suddenly froze. I thought to myself, "This is it, they're going to try to kidnap us."

The assassination of the U.S. ambassador and his deputy in Sudan had been a close call—perhaps too close. It was an honor for us to serve our government as its official representatives, but the honor also entailed risks. The diplomats from the major powers had become targets of unrestrained terror in many parts of the world. I wrote to Tom that we should consider leaving diplomatic service. It perhaps was wrong to risk our lives and the lives of the children. I thought often about the girls. They, too, could have been easily kidnapped by terrorists. Tom was an academic and we accepted the invitation to serve the U.S. government knowing that it was not permanent.

The children were confined to playing after school at our residence. Most playmates, who were children of other Americans or diplomats, were invited to our home, since we had a pool and it provided a pleasant and enjoyable diversion for everyone. During the Christmas holiday, we were able to take our only family vacation in Uganda. We traveled to Murchison Falls National Park, where, besides seeing the vast array of animals, we took a small boat trip on the Nile to view the falls which were seen by the first Europeans, Samuel Baker and his wife in 1864. There is a belief among the Acholi tribe that a ''spirit'' lives at the falls, to whom visitors must leave a gift as an appeasement for having entered his domain. As we were making a turn in the boat, our daughter Tina's shoe had come loose and somehow fell out. I cautioned her not to look for it. There were crocodiles lying two abreast on all the small islands in the river. They lay sleepily basking in the sun waiting for some interesting prey to come along. At last, the shoe was found in the bottom of the launch, and we had not left a gift either to the spirit or to the crocodiles. Later, I learned from reports of several missionaries that bodies with limbs missing and intestines protruding like sausages were thrown into the same Nile River. The crocodiles must have been well fed, for some technicians complained that at the Owen Dam on the Nile near Lake Victoria, bodies were continually being caught in the gates of the hydroelectric plant.

Fortunately, even during the shortages when Asian shops were closed, we were able to supply most of our needs. Tina, however, remembers that at her birthday party she received nothing but books. Toys and games were impossible to find in Kampala, but the stationery and book stores had remained open.

Among those Africans who worked at the embassy and residences, there were a number of black Kenyan nationals. A few of them decided they could no longer remain in Uganda. They feared for their lives.

The Kenya government was continually complaining to Uganda about the unsafe conditions for workers on the East African railroad. In February 1973, Kenya announced that over thirty Kenyan East African employees were missing in Uganda. Many of those who had disappeared were high-ranking officials of the joint regional company. A long-time Tanzanian friend who was employed by the East African Common Services in Kenya came on a business trip to Kampala. He told us during his visit how fearful Kenyans and Tanzanians were to travel to Uganda. Kenya-Uganda difficulties erupted in February 1976, when Amin verbally claimed a large portion of Kenyan territory for Uganda. The Kenyans, angered over the claims, allowed workers to stage a boycott on moving goods between Uganda and the Indian Ocean port of Mombasa. During the boycott, rallies were held at which Amin was hung in effigy. The controversy was finally calmed but Uganda was severely hurt by the trade embargo. Unfortunately, an innocent third party, the small country of Rwanda, suffered too since its imports and exports pass through Uganda and Kenya to and from ships at Mombasa.

Relations between Kenya and Uganda are still strained, for refugees pass every day across the border. Many are professionally trained people. Others are simple farmers. In June 1977, soldiers in uniform carrying arms crossed to Kenya and surrendered their arms to the authorities. After the tenth or eleventh assassination attempt on Amin's life in June 1977, a segment of the army had fled. With truck drivers in Kenya refusing to drive into Uganda because of safety hazards, the Uganda government now sends a plane weekly to London loaded with coffee, and returns carrying spare parts and luxuries such as shoes, Scotch, and cigarettes. Another coffee airlift was organized by an American-owned company from Entebbe to Djibouti, where the coffee is loaded on ships headed for Istanbul. Each plane load carries about $350,000 worth of coffee beans. This is now Amin's only source of foreign exchange.

I found it difficult to attend official functions where Amin was present. Some people found him amusing and jovial, but I could never dismiss the evil, cunning side of his nature. I had met many different sorts of people in Africa—some kind, dedicated, and genuine; others crafty, dishonest, and selfish. No one race has a monopoly on good or evil. I understood readily how Amin could dominate by fear but not by respect. It therefore puzzled me to

142

find some educated women attracted to him. I suppose a number of women are attracted by brute strength in men, but in the case of some of his coterie of female companions, I am sure that it was the pure excitement to be close to absolute power.

The women in Amin's life are too numerous to count. When we arrived, he had four wives. I asked politely at the Ugandan Foreign Office to call upon them but I was never given an answer. Some diplomats had been received by them, and at state or official functions, at least one would be chosen to sit beside her husband. Amin had chosen his wives with some political motive, in that they came from different tribes. At least one was a Christian. His first wife was said to have been a Kakwa like his father, but she evidently had been divorced to make way for Amin's fourth wife, Madina, from the Baganda tribe. According to the radio announcement at the time, Madina "had been given to him in appreciation of his generosity to the Baganda and because of the love he has shown them." The brother of Amin's wife Sarah (whom Amin renamed Mama Mariam) reported on the events that led to his sister's rise and fall from Amin's grace. He said that in 1961, Sarah failed to come home for more than a week. One day, a tall, powerful soldier came to Sarah's mother and said, "Mother, I am your son. I am Captain Idi Amin. I work in the army at Jinja. Your daughter Sarah is living with me." Sarah then married Amin and had seven children by him. Amin eventually divorced three of his wives, including Sarah, Kay, and Nora.

The fate of several of Amin's former wives is particularly indicative of his ruthless and callous rule. Shortly after being divorced by Amin in August 1974, his former wife Kay was found dead and dismembered in the trunk of a car. The official report from the government said that she had gone to a doctor for an abortion and had died of hemorrhaging. The police assumed that the doctor tried to hide her body in the car until he disposed of it, but fearing that he would be discovered, he tried to poison himself and his entire family. The doctor and two of his children were found dead. Kay, who had been a radio announcer before her marriage to Amin, was buried in her home area, but Amin did not attend the funeral.

There were, of course, other versions of the story. Some

claimed that Amin decided that Kay had been too close to her cousin Lieutenant Colonel Michael Ondoga, who had served as foreign minister and then disappeared. Kay demanded that Amin help her recover the body but Amin refused. She supposedly became angered and left Amin to live on her own. Amin then publicly announced his dissolution of his three marriages.

Another report says that Amin suspected Kay of having an affair with a Kampala doctor. When the doctor found that his garage had been broken into and Kay's body was stuffed in the trunk of his car, he knew that he would soon be taken by Amin's men. He then tried to poison himself and his family instead of submitting to certain torture and death.

In 1974, Sarah, who had been renamed Mariam, was involved in an automobile accident. She was visited in the hospital by Amin, who insulted her, claiming that she had been in the accident because she had not been living a life of sufficient discipline. She told him to leave, for she knew it had been his men who tried to kill her. Later, she managed to escape and join her brother, Wanume Kibedi, the former foreign minister who defected and was living in London. Nothing has been heard of the third wife, Nora, who was divorced.

Amin's Muganda wife, Madina, appeared at the ceremonies marking Amin's fourth year in power in January 1975. A month later, it was reported that she was badly beaten and her jaw broken. In July 1975, Amin took another wife, also named Sarah, a nineteen-year-old woman whom Amin said was a member of the "suicide revolutionary mechanized regiment." A report in 1977 was that Amin was enjoying a belated honeymoon with her.

In July 1973, Amin decreed the legalization of polygamy as a way of returning to "our cultural heritage." It really did not change the present social customs. A form of polygamy was being practiced in Uganda according to customary law. Yet, among a large segment of the Uganda population, the tradition had been to have only one official or chief wife. None of the others could match her position or stature, nor could they threaten to replace her.

Amin, however, used the issue of polygamy to present himself as a sexual superman. He bragged about the number of children he fathered and how he was able to keep all of his wives content.

144

Furthermore, he used his wives, who were from different tribes, as a political tool to indicate that he was intimately joined to all factions of the Ugandan population. His treatment of his wives, however, backfired on him. Some of them dared to challenge his actions. In the end, he had no respect for women and used them for his own purposes. After he was finished, he discarded them. His wives could not expect to be treated with dignity by Amin. One even lost her life.

The contacts that I had with Ugandan women indicated suspicion and dislike for Amin. I attended the last meeting of one of the active women's groups in Kampala. It was the last because Amin had issued a decree which brought all women's activities into one national women's organization. In terms of African political developments, this action was not startling. Many countries in Africa had one national women's organization which was either funded by the one political party or by the government. In Uganda, however, it met large-scale opposition. Private and church-related women's groups had been active in Uganda for many years. Although, as in all parts of Africa, women under the colonial system had not had the same opportunities for education as men, they had, nevertheless, succeeded in improving the situation in Uganda.

There were many women employed in the nursing and teaching fields. Many wives of high government officials worked professionally. Some ran commercial enterprises while their husbands drew government salaries. Most of these women worked to increase family income. Often, they had large, extended families to whom they had financial responsibilities. Others worked to fulfill professional expectations or interests. Through the missionaries and British expatriates, volunteer work was no stranger to the modern Ugandan society. Groups such as the YWCA, the Girl Guides, and the Red Cross were active and expanding organizations. Those involved in these programs had a vested interest and they resented the assumption that they would enthusiastically work for a new national organization. Elizabeth Bagaya, princess from Toro, who had trained as an advocate in England, was selected by Amin to chair the meeting to launch the national women's group. Many women leaders boycotted that meeting. Others who attended presented arguments criticizing the structure of the new group.

At the women's meeting that I attended in Kampala several arguments were presented. First, many considered the guidelines for participation in the national women's organization as racist. Their own organization was affiliated with an international group. It allowed foreign nationals and people of any race or color to be a part of the group. The new national organization would not permit any women's group except those which restricted membership to Ugandans. Others criticized the measure as limiting private participation. They feared government control and believed that only close followers of Amin would be permitted to hold leadership positions. Lastly, most of these women distrusted Amin. They were Christian and, therefore, suspicious of possible Moslem influence. They opposed polygamy and looked dimly on Amin's keeping of four wives. They feared Moslem inroads in their society. If their own husbands converted to Islam, they would want no part of a polygamist marriage. Nor did they wish to be subject to the easy divorce tradition among Moslem males.

I have heard many debates on the subject of traditional versus Westernized modern practices in regard to marriage, the dowry and polygamy. For those who advocate polygamy, the past is usually romanticized while the Christian and colonial era maligned. A return to the traditions of the past is usually the main thrust of the argument. It is true that many African men refused Christianity because it meant giving up their polygamous relationships. Some turned rather to Islam, which at least allowed them to keep four legal wives.

Women told me, however, that they are often used as scapegoats for African male anti-Western feelings. African women are often criticized for their modern dress, hair styles, or conduct. For men, however, this is no problem. They are permitted to use modern—and Westernized—ways, while women are supposed to remain on a quasivillage level.

While we were in Uganda, Amin had decreed that miniskirts were banned. Ugandan women were urged to return to African dress, especially on official or formal occasions. The Baganda women used their *basuti*, a long gown with full sleeves, which was really introduced to them by Christian missionaries. Elizabeth Bagaya set the style by wearing long gowns, many times of African materials. Her hair was braided in intricate patterns. She was stunning, but not everyone had her taste and good looks. Most women, including diplomats, lengthened their hems on their short dresses which were cooler and more comfortable for daytime wear.

I was impressed with the courage of the Ugandan women. Many of them put up a fight when their husbands were taken by Amin's soldiers. After their disappearances were announced, they continually pressured the government and Amin himself to provide answers concerning their husbands' fates. On one occasion, a conference of women called attention publicly to the numerous people who had vanished. The newspaper *Munno* reported on their action and within a few days, its editor, Father Kiggundu, was killed.

From February to April 1973, I was able to communicate with Tom only cryptically. Our phone calls were merely a way of hearing each other's voices. We could not exchange any real information. But I knew Tom's position well. He was convinced that Amin was not just a strong dictator, but a brutal tyrant. He wanted to reduce the American presence significantly. He hoped that he would be able to direct the operation of safely withdrawing as many U.S. citizens as possible from the country. There was a good possibility that he would be permitted to return for this sole purpose, and in early March, he told me that he would. In fact, at one point, he told me that he would be coming back to Kampala shortly.

One day, I received a telephone call from a Ugandan friend whom I had met in student days in New York in 1960. He had been living and working in Kampala but had not dared to contact us. Now he had heard a rumor that we were leaving. He was arranging for his young son to be baptized and asked me if I would be the godmother. I agreed. I was thrilled to see my friend again; but despite the usual joy that one feels at a christening, I was deeply moved by the aura of sadness that was present among his family and friends who gathered at his home afterwards.

147

I cannot even mention his name now for I am not sure if he has left Uganda. He apologized for having seemingly ignored our presence for so many months, but it was dangerous for Ugandans to be in contact with foreigners. His wife was not Ugandan, and he told me that she had been molested and beaten by Ugandan troops. He was frightened about her safety and, therefore, they rarely socialized outside their own family. It was unsafe to frequent the restaurants or clubs in town. They were overrun by Ugandan soldiers who often became unruly. They bullied civilians, taking whatever women they desired and threatening their escorts.

At the small family gathering after the christening, I was repeatedly questioned about American intentions. They had heard rumors circulating that the U.S. Embassy would be downgraded, or might even withdraw. They lamented the situation in Kampala but hoped that the U.S. government would stay. They had witnessed the departure of many professors, technicians, and even missionaries in the last few months. They themselves felt alone and threatened. Somehow, they felt that the mere presence of the foreign embassies was a comfort to the Ugandans who were suffering.

I was continually concerned that there might be an attempted coup or assassination attempt while we were in Kampala. I did not wish to be present, nor did I want to subject our children to the obvious confusion and bloodshed which would follow. At official functions, I was particularly aware that if any attempt was made to kill Amin, a guest might be caught in the crossfire. I remember reading accounts of a diplomatic function for the king of Morocco where suddenly machine guns fired. People were killed instantly, some cut right in half by the force of the guns. At one ceremony in Uganda, we arrived to find all the seats filled in the ambassadorial section, which was rather close to the presidential party. The chief of protocol for the Ugandan government requested that two Chinese diplomats who did not have ambassadorial rank give their seats to us. We saw them shake their heads in refusal. Rather than make a scene, we simply told the protocol chief that we would find seats further away in another section. I was actually pleased, for that placed us at a good distance from Amin and his entourage.

It was also depressing to see work stopped and unfinished. Our U.S. AID technicians were particularly affected, for some had spent six years on projects which, in the end, collapsed. Many of the schools faced severe problems. When they closed at Christmas vacation, some did not even know if they would reopen. In February, I accepted a speaking engagement at a Catholic girls' high school. The Sisters who directed the school were depressed, for they had lost many of the lay teachers. They had no Peace Corps volunteers, nor teachers provided by technical assistance programs from other foreign countries. Even they themselves felt their future uncertain. The spirit of these people was broken. They were holding on, and doing the best that they could under the circumstances, but all joy and enthusiasm had evaporated. I thought back on my former plans to come to teach in a similar school in Uganda as soon as I had finished college. I would have been alone then, but the climate had been so promising. The schools had meager supplies and little money, but there was a tremendous fervor for development and progress. Now, the atmosphere was dreary. It was almost without hope. The Sisters had worried constantly about the boarding students. There had been reports that roving bands of soldiers entered the grounds of another school and dragged off whatever girls pleased them. I recall the testimony of women students at the University of Makerere who said that when the soldiers tired of raping them, they used the barrels of their rifles.

As I prepared to leave, I tried to meet my responsibilities with regard to the residence. Materials had been ordered for recovering furniture, which I carefully locked away. The silver was counted and china inventoried. It, too, was locked in the storeroom. No one knew how long the residence would be unoccupied.

When questioned about my departure, I had to maintain that I was only going on leave, but everyone believed that I would not return. About the same time as my departure, the Italian ambassador Romanelli and his wife were leaving after a long tour of duty. There was the usual round of farewell parties for them. This also gave me a chance to see most of the diplomatic community before I left.

There were many, however, whom I had no chance of contacting. These were mostly Ugandans. I sent word to as many as I could, but there were some whom I would never see again. Joe Mubiru was one of these. I could not visit his grave, for it was not even acknowledged that he was dead. I could not express my sorrow to his wife who had gone into hiding.

The night of my departure from Uganda, I had gone to the home of the German ambassador and his wife, which was only two houses away from our residence. The children were with a trusted housekeeper and the residence was being guarded by a Ugandan policeman. I had received a phone call from the housekeeper informing me of some difficulty with the policeman, who refused to allow one of our friends to deliver some papers. The German ambassador, being a veteran diplomat, advised me to go with him in his car to the house—even though it was a very short walk. When we arrived at the gate, the policeman stopped the car pointing his rifle at us. I started to open the door but the German ambassador, fearing that this might frighten the policeman, quickly pulled me back. Realizing that the children were inside I had begun to panic. Finally, the policeman allowed the car to enter. As I was opening the front door to the house, the policeman snarled, "You're lucky I didn't kill your friend."

The girls and I left unceremoniously by plane from Entebbe airport the next morning, April 11, 1973. As the plane circled over the immense and swampy Lake Victoria, my last thought was that perhaps the body of my dear friend, Joe Mubiru, had been dumped like a sack of garbage into the waters that were the source of the Nile. It was an ugly farewell.

Ambassador and Mrs. Melady with daughters Christina and Monica on their last night together in Kampala, Uganda, February 8, 1973.

9: AMIN: THE AFRICAN HITLER

IN 1975 DENIS HILLS, A BRITISH TEACHER AND EXPERIENCED writer, was sentenced to death by a military tribunal in Uganda. His crime, supposedly, had been treason. The evidence was an unpublished manuscript in which he had described Amin as a "village tyrant." Amin announced that he wanted the British to deal with him directly on the issue before he would consider any act of clemency towards Hills. "I'm only fierce with British because I want these people to kneel down to my feet."

Britain then sent its foreign secretary to Kampala to see Amin. He brought with him a message from the Queen. Amin was thrilled. It was a superb theatrical performance. With a letter from Queen Elizabeth in his hand, Amin could then act as a benevolent ruler. He called Hills before him and said, "The execution order has been signed for tomorrow morning. But the Queen has written a letter to me, and the order will be reconsidered because the Queen is my friend."

Once again Amin had poked fun at the British. The Queen of England had capitulated before him, giving in to his wishes by writing in her own hand a letter concerning the fate of one of Britain's subjects. This was indeed a lofty achievement for a man who began as a lowly African recruit in the British colonial army.

Amin has a political shrewdness. He knew how to imitate the British officers when he worked to be promoted. When independence came, he learned the phraseology of African nationalists. Lacking any clear philosophy of his own, Amin turned to whatever knowledge he had gleaned from films and oral presentations to strengthen his leadership position.

In 1974, when the French film *General Idi Amin Dada* was made and shown in Western Europe and the United States, the audience found Amin hilarious. Some thought he was doing a comical impersonation of a "typical tyrant." He probably was impersonating—but he was quite serious.

Amin enjoys viewing films. His presidential palace supposedly has a library of films, many of which are old World War II stories. We can easily conclude that some of Amin's formulas are direct imitations of sensational war movies. Most of these American and British films about World War II portrayed the Allies in a favorable light, while discrediting the Nazi and Japanese enemies. Excessive militarization, war fever, brutality, espionage were all part of the dramatization of the tragedy of the long and costly war.

In a very simplistic way, Amin had theorized that the traditional "bad guys" in the film were fighting the British. Since he was supposed to be fighting the same enemy—the British—as the former colonial masters, then why not follow some of the same tactics, formulas, and phraseology of the Nazis and Japanese? He intended to be a strong, ruthless leader, for he himself had succeeded by brute strength, cunning, and falsehood. He would continue in the same pattern, but would add some of the trimmings of an equally strong dictator—Adolf Hitler.

Amin has used two special security units, the Public Safety Unit and the State Research Bureau, to carry out most of his terror unleashed on both the military and civilian population. He began first by staffing both these units with members of his own Kakwa tribe and other Nubians. While we were there, the Public Safety Unit was particularly dreaded. Now the State Research Bureau which is based in the president's office seems to be implicated in most of the disappearances and tortures. The former foreign minister, Wanume Kibedi, commented on these organizations in his letter to Amin. "The assassins are a small cabal of men owing direct loyalty to you personally. They are in general your ethnic kith and kin, and they operate in a number of security organizations which are mere fronts for their criminal activities." They are reported to dress in civilian clothes—often loud sports shirts and sunglasses. They drive in unofficial cars, whose license plates are sometimes covered. Most of all, they are feared by everyone.

The units act on direct orders from Idi Amin. They are given the task of eliminating all those whom Amin believes oppose him or threaten his regime. Now, the reasons for killing have degenerated into personal quarrels and insignificant offenses considered to be indications of political opposition. The units are given a wide range of power. They assume the power of life or

153

death. Some sources cited by the International Commission of Jurists claimed that lists of people were drawn up in 1971. About three thousand names were on it from every area of the country except Amin's own tribe. Names were crossed off this list as people were eliminated or pardoned. Others were added and the list is still being kept with the State Research Bureau.

The Public Safety Unit has transformed one of its armories at the police training center in Naguru into a prison. Methods of torture have been devised. Prisoners at Naguru are forced to put their heads in a metal truck wheel rim. One of the guards then stands on the neck of the prisoner and beats the metal rim with an iron bar so that the sound reverberates in the victim's head. At the same time, the prisoner is flogged with a *kiboko*, a whip made of dried hippopotamus skin.

Others are forced to crawl back and forth on stones in the courtyard on their hands and knees. One person testified that he saw a prison guard tie a string around one testicle of a prisoner and pull while the victim was being interrogated. Many times prisoners are forced to go without food or water. At Naguru they are taken every day to do exercises. If they fail to do them properly, they are whipped.

These killer squads organized by Amin are composed largely of members of his own tribe, Nubians and some Sudanese mercenaries. When the Public Safety Unit was formed, it was given the task of dealing with the roving bands of robbers called *kondos*. They were charged with shooting these robbers on the spot. In the beginning, when the disappearances were occurring, Amin often referred to the *kondos* and guerrillas who had been threatening the safety of private citizens. He often blamed the killings on these bands of criminals. But, gradually the people began to understand that it was really the special units formed in the police and in the military who were responsible for carrying out the murders.

Amin himself referred to the "boys" taking Benedicto Kiwanuka, the chief justice, who was subsequently murdered. These "boys" are Amin's collaborators who owe personal loyalty to him and have the blood of many of Amin's victims on their hands.

Similar special killer squads have been used in other regimes controlled by brutal tyrants. "Papa Doc" Duvalier of Haiti had his coterie of special police. The most famous in modern history was the SS or Schutzstaffel created by Hitler in 1925. The SS was supposedly a subordinate part of the Sturmabteilung (SA)—the brown-shirted storm troopers. Actually, it outranked all other groups for it was a select unit of hand-picked men who remained very close to the Führer and carried out many of his most dreaded policies. The membership was limited to those who represented the pure German race. Their backgrounds were varied—pig breeders, chauffeurs, as well as ex-officers and academics.

The other Nazi killer squad was the Gestapo, the secret state police which was eventually controlled by the SS. Both these dreaded names—the SS and the Gestapo—are well known to World War II movie viewers.

One of the characteristics of a totalitarian regime is the immediate and brutal elimination of all those who could constitute an opposition. In the year following Hitler's seizure of power, the SS, which then had full control over the Gestapo, compiled a central death list aimed at decimating the leadership of the rival SA. Others who were considered anti-Nazi personages were added to that list. Men were dragged from their beds and murdered. Others were herded into prisons and executed. The bloodletting began in Bonn and Munich and then spread to all the provinces. Extensive manhunts were formed to search for those who fled into the forests.

The German people were lulled into thinking that this brutal activity was better than the past period of the state's inaction. When Amin took over power in Uganda, the same occurred. The Kakwa and Nubian forces of the army systematically eliminated the Acholi and Langi army and police officers. In 1973, the former President Obote charged that the killing of thousands of Acholi and Langi amounted to genocide. However, these massacres, which were largely within the military and police force, were regarded by observers as an upheaval that usually occurs before a coup stabilizes itself.

Several terms that Amin uses are directly copied from the World War II era. For example, he has bestowed upon himself

Soldiers remove the body of a Ugandan executed by Amin's firing squad. Thousands attended the executions of Ugandans Amin suspected to be guerrillas.

United Press International

the title of field marshal. This military rank has hardly been heard since the World War II era. The other term is the suicide revolutionary mechanized regiment, which Amin formed to supposedly train fighters such as the Japanese kamikaze pilots who were ready to perform suicide crashes on the enemy. His latest wife is a member of Amin's most recent military creation.

It is difficult to compare the highly scientific and efficient appearance of the Nazi regime with the disorderly and chaotic rule of the present government in Uganda. Both, however, were guided by the direct personality of the supreme ruler. In October 1938, Hitler articulated the Nazi concept of legality: "All means, even if they are not in conformity with existing laws and precedents, are legal if they subserve the will of the Führer." Uganda is ruled by a series of directives and decrees handed down by the President. Amin's former foreign minister, Wanume Kibedi, called it "the era of one-man government which has now become a permanent feature of Amin's rule." In a decree in May 1972, Amin gave immunity to the government—and therefore, the army —for any criminal prosecution. This prevented any legal means to be used to make the army or police responsible for the many murders. The rule of law was quickly and definitely abandoned.

Furthermore, Amin relies on oral reports and directives. E. B. Rugumayo, who was minister of education while we were in Uganda, described Amin's method of governing when he reported to the International Commission of Jurists. "Since most of his ministers are what one might term technocrats, he finds them too complicated and uninteresting, although they are the people who should actually give him correct information. Instead he has to have recourse to people of his own level of intelligence and caliber. In effect, these are the people who rule the country; the illiterate and semiliterate army officers who have recently been drafted into the service. Practically all of them get their information by word of mouth and get directives from their superiors verbally. Since little is written down, once said, there is little or no follow-up to change the plan or check the facts."

Hitler used to say, "a single idea of genius is worth more than a whole lifetime of conscientious office work." His dislike for the discipline of regular and serious work was called his "bohemian" trait. Hitler, like Amin, tired of the rigors of departmental reports, growing uninterested in many facets of the government. Only after he had formulated his aggressive nationalistic plans for Germany did he once more feel the intoxication of power. War was the answer to his personal success.

Various biographies of Hitler discuss his personal transformation as a soldier. Previously, he had been a floundering youth failing to attain certain goals and lacking interest in a steady profession. The business of war gave him personal strength. He excelled as a soldier, never grumbling about hardships. He developed a burning desire for victory and the destruction of the enemy. Later, as the supreme commander of the Third Reich, Hitler basked in the adulation given to him as he led triumphant forces across Europe.

Amin also has war fever. He must constantly wage war in order to attain the status he desires. First, it was the Economic War. His targets were the Israelis, the Asians, and the British imperialists. Having won these wars, he threatened and bullied his neighbors Tanzania and Kenya. At one point, one of his special units began stopping all cars that had registration plates of Kenya. In one instance, a truck driver and his helper from Kenya were loading bananas when the police questioned them on their documents. They were told that there had been a ban on the banana export and were taken to the prison for smuggling. They were beaten severely with a whip and then held overnight. During the night they heard a series of shots. The next day they were asked to clean the back of a truck which was coated with human blood.

Joachim C. Fest, a German journalist and radio broadcaster, once wrote in his book, *The Face of the Third Reich*, that Hitler "was no more than a beer-cellar agitator of demonic proportions who discounted all moral evaluation and saw the harassing problems that had been placed in his hands in the hazy perspective of the Munich local politician." In somewhat the same manner, Denis Hills, the British writer and teacher, wrote that Amin rules like a "village tyrant, by fear."

Hitler had become a mystical and idolized hero by 1938. He was superhuman with an infallibility that one dared not to question. He demanded listeners and never tolerated objections. As time wore on, he became more and more obstinate and arrogant.

When Amin first came to power, he spoke of himself as a professional soldier, not a politician. He humbly listened to his cabinet officials and various ethnic and interest groups. His taste for power grew rapidly, and soon he became accustomed to seeing himself in the front page and on television news. His ego swelled. The suggestions and programs outlined by various ministers were soon rejected, for Amin had little time for such painstaking details. He developed rule by decree. When challenged, he acted brutally to put an end to a criticism or disagreement. We had heard that Amin often would turn to his henchmen and say, "Finish him." The word "finish" meant kill. It was the only way Amin knew how to silence those who objected. When he answered the inquiries of the Minister of Health Kyemba on the fate of Mrs. Dora Bloch, the Israeli hostage, Amin said, "They have already finished her."

In the first two years of Amin's reign, people frequently referred to him as just another one of the many authoritarian heads of state in the world. Over half of the countries in the world have authoritarian governments. Consequently, there was a reluctance to distinguish between Amin and other authoritarian leaders.

It was indeed unfortunate that in 1971 and 1972, despite numerous reports on atrocities, Amin was regarded by many as merely another dictator. We finally classified him as a brutal tyrant by late 1972 when we saw his total commitment to torture and death as a routine means to perpetuate his regime.

The same was true of the early evaluations of Hitler. "Strong man, folk hero," is the classification that was given by many to Hitler in 1935 as he was scheming to launch the "final solution" against the Jews. In the case of Amin, the realization that he is a brutal tyrant came sooner than with Hitler. By the time that Amin called for his own version of the "final solution" against the State of Israel in his infamous 1975 address at the United Nations, there were few who would deny he was a murderer. This is totally different from being an authoritarian leader. There are strong rulers today who are serving their people. It is an insult to them to, in any way, place them in the same category as Hitler and Amin. Even among the group of rulers who are continually violating the human rights of their own people, Amin still leads all others in the scale of his brutality. The Nigerian playwright, Wole Soyinka, wrote a letter to the magazine *Africa* in which he said:

> There has to be a ceiling of tolerance even for a people who have become lately inured to the language of violence from their rulers in all its dehumanizing variations. Calculated genocide in Burundi, selective sadism chez Marechal Bokasa, sweeping liquidations by the latest Papa Doc of the African continent, Macias Nguema of Equatorial Guinea, these are lesser known examples of brutalized societies on the other side of that already overgenerous level of toleration. Idi Amin, of course, reigns supreme. He is in a class by himself.

We have heard many contend that Amin really does not know a fraction of the people who have been killed by his soldiers and police. He supposedly has given them such free rein in the power of arrest and execution that much has taken place without his knowledge. At a recent meeting of exiled Ugandan Christian bishops, we heard one say that "Amin set the machinery into action and now he cannot stop that machinery. . . . Most things he does not know. The State Research Unit has a free ticket."

The same was said of Hitler. Richard Grunberger, in his book, *The 12-Year Reich*, wrote, "Many Germans, persuaded of the state's preemptive claim on citizens' lives, absolved the head of state of culpability for its crimes. Moving within the most tightly structured governmental system in Western history, they nevertheless managed to dissociate centrally directed atrocities from the man at the centre—an attitude of many that found expression in such cant-phrases as 'It's all the fault of the little Hitlers' or 'If only Adolf knew about this.' "

We have even heard people say that Amin is often misunderstood by his Nubian bodyguards. When he is tired or angered, he dismisses whomever he is interrogating saying, "I am finished with you." His henchmen take the word "finish" literally and lead the person out to be killed. Increasing evidence by accounts of those who have worked with Amin and then defected are disproving these theories as, more and more, Amin is implicated in the minute details of the large-scale killings. The younger brother of one of Amin's wives, Francis Nyende Kibedi, stayed in Uganda after both his sister and his brother, who had served as foreign minister, had defected. He still trusted Amin and did not wish to believe all of the accusations. One day, he too was arrested and brought before Amin. There he was charged by Amin with collaborating with exiles. Amin barked to his aides that the boy was dangerous and ordered them to take him for questioning. After the interrogation, Kibedi was placed in Makindye Prison. Later, he was taken again to see Amin. The room was filled with newsmen, television cameras, and Kibedi's parents. Amin showed him to the journalists to prove that he was still alive. Amin said nothing of his imprisonment to the press and told a fictitious story to the young man's parents of the reasons for Kibedi's arrest. "As I heard him lying," Kibedi wrote later, "my trust and hope died as suddenly as he had come into our lives." As soon as Kibedi was released, he slipped across the border to Kenya.

Once killing is sanctioned, it opens the door for senseless brutality. In Nazi Germany, political and military rivals tried to have each other arrested. Members of the SS could trust no one. For some, it was standard practice to enter a building with a revolver cocked. The ordinary citizens were urged to be vigilant and to report all infractions to the proper authorities. Quarreling neighbors looked for ways of denouncing each other. There were even situations where one family member handed over another. The crimes reported ranged from grumbling about the regime to frequenting Jewish shops. A very easy way to eliminate a rival for a position was to prove some Jewish association in the past.

In Uganda, army and police members wield so much power that they can easily decide the fate of any person in the country. Besides carrying out the expressed orders of Amin, soldiers have been known to arrest anyone for any reason—to take property, money, a woman, or even to settle some minor quarrel. In 1972, a district commissioner and the hotel manager in Tororo both disappeared. They had had a dispute with some soldiers over

161

payment for their drinks. In 1974, a man named Wilson James Byakika gave a signed statement to the International Commission of Jurists in which he described how he had been assigned with Godfrey Kiggala to look after an official North Korean delegation. Amin personally left instructions for them to wait at a hotel for further communication. Amin did not telephone. Instead he sent his bodyguards to arrest the two men.

Byakika told the story: "Godfrey and I were tied up with ropes, thrown into the boot of the car, and driven to a forest about thirty miles from Kampala, where we were shot. Godfrey died. I was left for dead, but I survived. I walked many miles before I obtained assistance. . . . I believe that the reason we were arrested and ordered to be shot was that Godfrey Kiggala was believed by General Amin to be a rival for the attention of a lady friend, and that I was arrested simply because at the time I was working with Kiggala in looking after the North Korean trade delegation, and was, therefore, associated in General Amin's mind with him. I was not a personal friend of Kiggala."

In the early propaganda of the Nazi regime, people heard promises of scouring out all of the old corrupt practices. The people who came to power in 1933 were supposed to be dedicated. Yet, soon corruption was once again rampant. Nazi leaders readily accepted castles, estates, and shares in businesses. Joseph Goebbels, head of the Nazi propaganda ministry, procured palatial residences by dispossessing Jews. There are tales that as soon as Jews were sent to concentration camps, a Nazi officer would come with his wife to try on the clothes hanging in the closet. Although contents of the apartments were supposed to be auctioned off by the state, the officer in charge would often quietly have a truck pick up what he wanted from the furnishings before an inventory was taken. Aryanization was a means of profit for many. When Jewish shops were closed, there were three or four applicants for the business. When they were reopened, some new owners showed much higher profit margins than the former Jewish shopkeepers.

After the expulsion of the Asians in Uganda, the shops were closed. A committee was composed to inventory the businesses and parcel them out to new owners. The civilian committee had hardly begun its work when a military committee was suddenly placed in charge of the major urban areas. Long lines of applicants appeared at the office of this committee. In the end, Amin himself had a great deal to say about who occupied the shops, for many of his close military officers and their families received the keys to these Asian businesses.

The supreme leader is supposed to be above corruption. The image of Hitler that was portrayed to the public was that of selfless servant of the people. Amin, too, claims that he is the poorest man in Uganda. Both Hitler and Amin not only turned their backs on the large-scale corruption but they encouraged it. First of all, they ignored the large-scale corrupt practices and crime and instead called public attention to the small petty infractions. In the Nazi regime, people were punished for not saluting or for listening to foreign broadcasts. In Uganda, businessmen caught hoarding or overcharging were flogged publicly. Nevertheless, African traders have taken advantage of the shortages and charged two or three times as much as the Asians. Some claim that the Nubians or Sudanese mercenaries who are involved with shops in Kampala see their businesses as quick ways to become rich. They have no idea how long the regime will last and want to make their profits as quickly as possible.

In Nazi Germany, particularly in the elite SS, corruption was uncovered but ignored. For example, officers who were found profiteering or looting were merely transferred. When a team of investigators was about to look into practices at a concentration camp, the authorities massacred forty thousand Jewish inmates in one day to assure that they would not present incriminating evidence.

Amin never acted on the clear investigation of the murders of the two Americans, Stroh and Siedle. The officers involved are still in leadership positions in Uganda. Amin set up a Commission of Inquiry into the disappearances in 1974. The report of this commission was issued in the following year. It named 308 people who had disappeared. Amin promised that those senior police and army officers implicated in the disappearances would be tried by a military tribunal. Naturally people were frightened to testify against these men. In July 1975, Ali Towilli, former head of the Public Safety Unit, and the senior assistant commissioner of police, Obura, were acquitted on charges of kidnapping a woman police constable.

It is essential for a tyrannical leader to hold the absolute loyalty of at least the privileged elite of his troops who guard and protect him. In Nazi Germany, army service was made particularly attractive. Army personnel received special rations, uniforms, and even entertainment. The SS corps was particularly favored. To many, it was a hitherto impossible chance of rising up the social ladder of acceptability. The elite unit was of pure-blooded Germans and they received many more luxuries than the ordinary troops. The SS was even provided with medically supervised brothels where German women could be impregnated by "racially pure" men. The officers were awarded estates, while the other ranks received farmsteads.

In Uganda, shortages occur frequently. Some items are constantly rationed. Even while we were there, sugar was a much sought item. Two leading Asian families owned and operated the sugar plantations and processing plants near Jinja. When they departed, the plants closed. No longer could the local people obtain Ugandan sugar. A supply was ordered from Kenya, but as soon as word passed through the city of Kampala that a particular store had sugar, long lines appeared in the streets. The soldiers, however, did not have to worry. They were always carefully and adequately supplied. They had first choice before the masses of Ugandan people. The army also took over the Entebbe golf club for its own social and recreational purposes. In effect, the military overran practically all of the hotels, restaurants, and clubs in town. They not only had the money to spend, but everyone else was afraid to expose themselves to their company lest they accidentally fall into an argument with a gun-wielding soldier. Most Ugandans knew that they should never even look at a soldier's lady friend, for they could be shot instantly. Amin often bestows gifts of land as rewards or enticements for loyalty. In August 1975, Amin sent a telegram to Arafat, the head of the Palestinian Liberation Organization, notifying him that Uganda had allotted 5,000 *fedan* of land to be cultivated by Palestinian Arabs. This land would be considered PLO property.

The Nazi regime in Germany forcefully maligned intellectuals and academics. Nazi leaders not only purged Jews, Social Democrats, and others opposed to their power from the university faculties, they continually assaulted the intellectual, saying that higher education separated one from the people. Academics were accused of selfish acquisition of knowledge. Student enrollment at the universities declined, not only because of the vile campaign against the purpose of higher education, but because university professors were either removed or resigned, causing havoc with university programs.

Amin has launched a similar attack on intellectuals. In 1922, a small technical school on Makerere Hill outside of Kampala, Uganda, had become a college, and thus, laid the foundations for a center of higher learning in East Africa. In that year, there were twelve African students and a handful of professors. In 1972, we were present for the fiftieth anniversary celebration of a university which had indeed become a fine institution with a distinguished reputation. Thirty-five hundred students were being trained in medicine, law, education, agriculture, veterinary science, and other fields. There was no doubt that this institution, once associated with London University and now an autonomous national university, had a great deal to celebrate. There was, however, a terrible cloud that darkened the events. Its vice chancellor and chief administrative officer had disappeared.

Much has happened to the university since that anniversary date. Many foreign faculty members left. The Asians were expelled. Fine scholars and students from other parts of Africa were reluctant to risk their lives in a country in which no one's safety could be reasonably guaranteed. Finally, even many Ugandan professors themselves fled. Indeed the spirit of the students was dampened but not entirely broken. In fact, twice they staged the only public demonstrations against Amin.

The first time was when the Libyan leader, Colonel Qaddafi, came to address the students at the university when he was on a state visit to Uganda. During the speech, Colonel Qaddafi spoke vehemently against the Jews and Christians. The students protested in silence by walking out of the audience.

The next student demonstration occurred in 1976. It was fully documented by the International Commission of Jurists. Captain Serwagi, the sports officer of the Ugandan army, was noted for his continual abuse of both university students and secondary school students. He particularly enjoyed boasting of sexual feats with girl students. Once, while inspecting the marching of secondary students, he incurred the anger of one male student who slapped him. Serwagi opened fire, killing the student and injuring several others.

In March 1976, three soldiers arrived at the university campus. They hunted down and killed a student named Paul Serwanga. He was supposedly a suitor of a girl in whom the army captain Serwagi was interested. When they heard the news, the students were bitter and decided that they must take some action. On March 6, thousands assembled in the main square of the university. They marched down through the town singing "Save us from Amin, save us from the murderers." Many others joined in the march. Police officers tried to persuade them to end their demonstration, but student leaders shouted that they no longer recognized Amin's government. Finally, the students returned to the university.

Within a few days, Amin came with many of his top ministers and army officers to the campus. Most lecturers and students refused to attend the meeting. Amin then announced that he would set up a commission to investigate the death of the student Serwanga, but he instructed university authorities to discipline the students. On August 3 and 4, 1976, the police raided the campus and took custody of several hundred students. Within a few days, 130 bodies of students were found near the campus. They had been tortured before being murdered. Another 80 have since been killed in prison.

Before his coup, Amin and President Obote did not agree on military promotions. In fact, Amin blocked several of Obote's candidates because Amin claimed that they had not had experience. These candidates had received formal training and education. They had not come up the ranks as Amin. They were also mostly Langi and Acholi.

In the beginning period after the coup, Amin courted the educated elite, hoping to use them in manning his government. He

166

soon found that he could not work with them, for they operated on an entirely different plane than Idi Amin. On one occasion, Amin claimed that his speed was much too fast. Most of his ministers could not keep up with him. Amin said, "Sometimes people mistake the way I talk for what I am thinking. I never had any formal education—not even a nursery school certificate. But, sometimes I know more than Ph.D.'s because as a military man I know how to act. I am a man of action."

Manipulation of the news is a characteristic of totalitarian states. In Nazi Germany, knowledge of the atrocities in concentration camps was widespread but very vague. An aura of secrecy surrounded the topic of the camps, but just enough was made known to the public to instill fear and dread. A stereotyped explanation of deaths that occurred in the camps was "shot while trying to escape." Joseph Goebbels, who managed Nazi propaganda, believed that propaganda did not have to be intelligent, just successful.

In Uganda, the news reports are almost always directed or composed by Amin himself. In these reports, the facts and circumstances are twisted and misconstrued. Amin himself lies constantly. In the first few years, there was a cleverness about the methods of revealing only partial information on the brutality of the regime. The disappearances, for instance, kept people in a wondering state. Nothing could be proven. Were the disappearances a result of the growing bands of robbers, or was the government responsible? Were the missing people really dead? Were they in prison or in hiding? An aura of mystery pervaded the country. It engendered fear, but at the same time, people did not know who they should fear—the government or the robbers? Then to add to the confusion, Amin began talking of Zionist and imperialist guerillas.

Radio Uganda often reported people killed in car accidents when really they were shot. The deaths of Father Kiggundu in 1973 and Bishop Luwum in 1977 attest to these lies. Shootings and explosions during the night were often camouflaged by statements about army maneuvers or detonation of bombs. When Mrs. Bloch, the Israeli hostage, was dragged from her hospital room and killed, the Uganda government claimed that she had

167

been returned to the airport before the Israeli attack. A favorite technique of the Uganda regime is to refuse access to the bodies of the killed. In this way, the disappearance forever remains a mystery. At least in Nazi Germany, in a few cases, the ashes of those killed in camps were sent to the nearest relative.

Both Hitler's and Amin's regimes attacked the Christian churches. The hero worship of the Führer and Nazi institutions has been described as neo-paganism. In the major ceremonies of life—birth, marriage, and death—Nazi leaders attempted to de-Christianize the rituals, instituting formulas of the state. Yet, at the same time, Nazi leaders attempted to deepen the religious differences between Christian and Jews in their attempt to secure the support, or at least nonopposition of the Christian churches to their pogrom of the Jewish people. When a bishop used his position to denounce Nazi programs, the Hitler regime arranged for the killing of three of his priests. The death of these priests went relatively unnoticed, but the Nazi regime carefully avoided persecuting the bishop directly, for it may have elevated him to hero status. The Christian churches were persecuted just enough so as to instill fear, but not full-scale resistance.

Amin's war against the church is well known, for unlike the Nazi regime, a bishop was killed for his forthright remarks about the excesses of Amin's policies. During an interview in June 1977, Amin denied any responsibility for the death of Archbishop Luwum. "I am not responsible at all. I am not against any person who is against me. . . . I believe strongly in God." The evidence on the Luwum case clearly implicates Amin. Even if he did not personally take part in Luwum's killing, even if he did not explicitly issue the orders for his death, he would still be responsible for the monster he has created. It disgusts us to watch this man meekly turn to his interviewers and blithely claim his innocence as a hardened criminal pleading for the sympathy of the court. There is no distinction between right and wrong. Ministers who have now fled report telephoning Amin about various disappearances, or alleged killings, in hope that Amin would respond with horror to search out the culprits who perpetrated these crimes. In all cases, Amin would calmly answer, "Is that so? I will look into the matter." When atrocities were being committed in the concentration camps of Germany, those in the regime never admitted it. When told of the massacre of men and women outside his headquarters building, Field Marshal Ernst Busch ordered his aide to "draw the curtains."

The use of sex to discredit and ruin a person's reputation was often used in Nazi Germany. There were the typical poison-pen letters to soldiers alleging the infidelity of their wives. There were jealous wives who could destroy a husband's position by proving he had a Jewish lover. Within the government itself, there were instances where sex was used to purge high-ranking officials from their posts. One such official's wife was discovered to have run a call-girl service. Another official was charged with homosexuality.

Amin seems to have a fixation on sex. He proves his masculinity by displaying his wives and children, but he also dwells on some of the sordid aspects of sexuality. In speaking about the economy, Amin once added, "No one is afraid here. It's like Uganda girls. I tell them to be proud, not shy. It's no good taking a girl to bed if she is shy—do you get my point?" He lectures soldiers and students on the spreading of venereal disease. One time at Makerere University, Amin spoke to the students on hygiene, "You must make yourself very smart, very clean, very healthy. I find that the VD is very high. If you are a sick man, sick woman, you had better go to the hospital, make yourself clean or you will find that you will infect the whole population. I like you very much and I don't want you spoiled by gonorrhea."

Sex is also used by Amin to discredit. He sometimes accuses his foes of spreading "political gonorrhea." Perhaps the most horrible example of the depths to which Amin would go in defaming a person's reputation is the episode involving Elizabeth Bagaya.

Not long after arriving in Kampala, we had the opportunity of meeting Elizabeth Bagaya. Besides being a tall and glamorous beauty, she was also a princess. Her father had been king of Toro, a region in Western Uganda containing the magnificent snow-capped Mountains of the Moon. Miss Bagaya was refined and intelligent, as well as worldly wise. In New York, she had been a fashion model, and in England, she had studied law. In

169

1972, she held the position of roving ambassador in Amin's government. She was often given difficult missions both in foreign and domestic affairs, and she usually accomplished these feats with aplomb. Her wit and grace made her the star attraction at receptions and dinners, and she seemed to be admired and well liked by everyone. She lived very near our residence, and the day before Margaret's departure, she invited her for tea. It was a pleasant hour in which Miss Bagaya steered gracefully away from any political subjects. In February 1974, Lieutenant Colonel Michael Ondoga was relieved from his post as foreign minister. In March, his body was found in the Nile River. Elizabeth Bagaya was selected to take his place. She flew to New York for the United Nations General Assembly meeting in the fall of 1974. She made a stunning performance at the UN, where she appeared in flowing gowns and African hairdos, castigating people like U.S. Secretary of State Henry Kissinger on his neglect of Africa. When she returned from her foreign trip, she was brought before Amin and accused of squandering Ugandan money on expensive clothing. Furthermore, Amin publicly accused her of having "made love to an unknown European in a toilet" at Orly airport in Paris.

In December, Amin brought Miss Bagaya before the TV cameras to prove that she was still alive. She was then placed under house arrest in her home in Kampala. In January 1975, the Ugandan official newspaper printed a half-length nude picture of Elizabeth Bagaya. The picture, the paper said, was taken when she was modeling and "plunged into an abyss of immorality." Eventually, Miss Bagaya was released and appeared in Kenya. She now lives in exile.

We were astonished one time to find a Käthe Kollowitz drawing on the walls of an American diplomat's home in Africa. One does not usually find such treasures displayed in houses that serve as temporary homes for two or three years. The artist was noted for her depiction of victims of the German concentration camps. When we looked at the anguish of the faces of the subjects of that drawing, we thought of the holocaust victims that had inspired the artist's work. It is difficult to look back upon those nightmare years in history. without feeling the chills and shudders of horror

Princess Elizabeth, former foreign minister of Uganda.

and disgust at the depths to which humanity descended. Thousands upon thousands were rounded up, stripped of all clothing, and lined up in front of long ditches. As they were executed, they fell layer upon layer into the mass graves. Then, gas chambers were used as "more pleasant" means of extermination. Into these chambers, seven hundred to eight hundred people would be crammed naked. In a half hour, all was over. When the doors opened, the bodies were still erect for there had been no room to fall. Workers then checked the tossed out bodies looking in mouths or genital organs for hidden money or diamonds. Gold teeth were hammered out and the bodies were then sent to the ovens to be burned. Among those who escaped immediate death, there was always the threat of starvation and torture.

As the Nazi soldiers swept over Eastern Europe, they carried their brutality to others. In reprisal for an assassination of a Nazi leader, a whole village in Czechoslovakia was razed to the ground. All male inhabitants over fifteen were shot. Women were sent to concentration camps and the children were dragged off to orphanages.

While the numbers have not reached the proportions of the pogrom against the Jewish people in Nazi Germany, tales of atrocities and mass killings in Uganda are no less cruel. In 1975 and 1976, some of the most harrowing testimonies were given to the International Commission of Jurists about the most recent atrocities. A businessman who had been detained in Naguru prison told how one or two prisoners were called out after a shooting had occurred. The prisoners were given a car axle and told to beat the dead man's head to a pulp. Then the prisoners were ordered to lie down in the blood and gore of the dead person. One prisoner told how he was put in charge of the jobs of other prisoners, "I had to give little jobs to the prisoners as well as smashing heads and loading bodies: things like cleaning the blood from the vehicles, supervising picking up eyes, teeth, and broken parts of heads, and making sure the blood was covered with dirt. We used to make a small hole just behind the toilet for the eyes, teeth, and broken skulls and cover it up." This same man had been told by guards at the prison that things used to be worse.

"They used to slash the prisoners' bellies open with machetes and put their hands in and pull out the intestines."

Another prisoner described how one hundred girls were arrested for wearing miniskirts. The girls' heads were shaven and one was singled out and gang raped.

In December 1974, a Ugandan schoolmaster fled the country with a harrowing tale to tell. He was arrested and imprisoned at Makindye in Kampala. During the night he and seven other men were given hammers and led to a cell with twenty-seven people. Some of them had broken limbs, others were bleeding from wounds. The soldiers then ordered the prisoners to kill the men in the cell. "We started hitting them on the heads with the hammers and all of them were killed." The soldiers just laughed, leaving them in the cell with those whom they had killed. The next day, the schoolmaster was taken to a forest camp where he saw two men beheaded by a guard. "We saw him [the guard] lick the blood from the knife." Then the two prisoners were ordered to butcher the corpses and the meat was cooked over a fire. The teacher told how they were hungry and ate shamefully. Some of them vomited and were beaten by the guards. After a few days, the same procedure was carried out. This time, eight victims were beheaded and butchered. The next night, the schoolmaster escaped while the guards were drinking.

In 1975, a large-scale massacre took place at a village in the Karamoja province of Uganda. Several soldiers knocked on the door of a village house. They had been drinking and intended to have sexual intercourse with the man's wife. As they pushed their way into the house, the man struck one of the soldiers dead with an iron bar. When the others ran back to the barracks, they said that they had been ambushed by guerrillas at the village. The army battalion was then sent to the village where they attacked the villagers with automatic weapons and set fire to their houses.

In the Hitler and Amin regimes, one atrocity has led to another greater act of violence. In both cases, the leaders have endorsed the holocaust as a proper activity to be sponsored by the state. The atmosphere in the first days of Hitler was such an obscenity that it is difficult to comprehend unless you have witnessed the same suffering. We had studied the brutality of Hitler but only

173

began to know it when we saw it taking place before our very eyes in Uganda.

By the time the world community began to sense the total brutality of Hitler, he had started the final process of total destruction. In the case of Amin, the destruction has been for the most part limited to Uganda. It is only a few hours before midnight when the holocaust will deepen within the tortured country of Uganda and spread its destructive fires to other parts of the continent and perhaps the world. Will midnight come!

10: WHAT CAN BE DONE ABOUT THE NEW HITLER

IDI AMIN DADA OF UGANDA IS RESPONSIBLE FOR THE TORTURE and murder of over one hundred thousand Ugandans. An admirer of the late Nazi Adolf Hitler, he gives an ugly impersonation of many of Hitler's characteristics and methods. The main focus of his brutality has been the black people of Uganda.

Portrayed by some as a comic, dismissed by others as a madman, this cruel and vicious tyrant is still not taken seriously by the world community.

Idi Amin Dada came to power in Uganda in 1971. He was a "misfit" of his country. Coming from a small, neglected tribe of northern Uganda, he had no sense of values either of the old or new order. He found purpose in the military and through his overpowering size and ruthless ways, he was able to ascend to the highest rank in the Uganda army.

Amin's rule has been by fear and diversion. The killings have not only been numerous, but brutal and torturous. To divert attention from the local holocausts that he has conducted, Amin has cleverly used international incidents like the expulsion of the Asians, the hijacking of the Air France plane in 1976, and the threats against American and British citizens living in Uganda in 1977.

His anti-Semitic thesis has been as vicious as that of Hitler. There are those who suggest that he is an African hero. Yet, he has shown no respect for African tradition nor has he made any effort to help the poor and afflicted of his country.

There is a real difference between authoritarian rule and tyranny. Most of the Third World countries faced with the battle against the triple curse of poverty, illiteracy, and disease have adopted authoritarian systems of government so they can win this battle quickly, but they still have a fundamental respect for human rights.

But Amin's Uganda is the example of ongoing genocide. His rule must be placed in the same category of the recent Hitler and Stalin terror eras. And like the two earlier tyrants, Amin espouses the same evils that led to a world war.

The first manifestations of his brutality occurred shortly after his overthrow of the Obote government in January 1971. There were reports of many deaths in Uganda in the first six months of his regime. World opinion in 1971 and 1972 tended to dismiss those deaths as part of the consolidation that occurs after a military coup d'état. Instead, it was the prologue of a reign of torture, oppression, and death.

His early embrace of brutality was found in his statements and actions on Israel and the Jewish people. He endorsed the worst forms of anti-Semitism that included the Nazi genocide. He has continued to copy the man that he admires—Adolf Hitler.

Since he was able in the early months of his reign to follow Hitler-like actions with the Jews without suffering any serious world reactions, he then began to brutalize another minority group, the Asians. These brown-skinned residents of Uganda were brutalized in 1972 in such a way that there are few recent parallels on the suffering of a minority group caused by one man.

The most horrible acts of murder have been against his own people. The black Ugandan people have suffered the most. It has been personally difficult for us to write some of these chapters where we have recounted the torture and death of thousands of Ugandans who included some of our friends.

The response of the world until most recently has been one of inaction. As the world media began to report Amin's brutality in 1972, there was growing discussion of his tyranny. No country took any real action even to indicate its displeasure until 1973, when the United States closed its diplomatic mission there. The British followed the U.S. example in 1976.

Amin has been received by heads of state and in 1975 received two standing ovations at the United Nations. In the 1971–76 period, no country, and no world body was prepared to give the leadership to any action that would stop the brutality against the people of Uganda.

There were a few voices that spoke against him on the world scene and they included African leaders like Julius Nyerere of Tanzania, Seretse Khama of Botswana, and Kenneth Kaunda of Zambia. President Ford in 1975 and President Carter in 1977 assailed repeatedly Amin's disgusting record. But the neighboring African countries and the Western world took no real concrete action to stop the massive violations of human rights in Uganda.

Local representatives of the People's Republic of China expressed disgust for Amin to us in 1972 in Uganda. There was no support on the international scene from the Chinese for the tyrant of Uganda.

Amin has been supported by several external sources. They include the Soviets, who have provided him with extensive amounts of military equipment; the Libyan government of Colonel Qaddafi, who has supplied him with financial aid; the Palestine Liberation Organization and allied groups, who supply personnel and counsel, and assorted extremist groups throughout the world.

There is one world organization that does have the mandate to act—the United Nations. Until 1977, the record of the UN in regard to Amin has been disappointing. The UN adopted in Paris the Declaration on Human Rights in 1955, and the UN subcommission on Human Rights was established to protect the rights of men and women everywhere. Yet in 1977, the UN Commission voted not to review the matter of the obvious gross violations of human rights in Uganda. And this came less than two years after Amin was welcomed at the UN and given two standing ovations!

Our bewilderment over the lack of international action is one of the main reasons for us to set forth the ugly record of Amin in this book. Perhaps in this way we can help to end the suffering of the Ugandan people.

There are essentially three actions that one can contemplate in regard to Amin. One, of course, is silence or ineffective verbal protest. The enormity of Amin's crimes against human rights is such that silence or ineffective verbal protest is an indecent rejection of our responsibilities in the world family.

Some have proposed unilateral intervention by another country so that Amin could be overthrown. While his crimes have been outrageous, we are opposed to any such unilateral action, especially by the United States, to oust him from office as it lacks sanction in the international community.

We do advocate forceful international action by the United Nations to bring an end to the suffering of the Ugandan people under Amin. The United Nations has the authority and the clear responsibility to act.

In the past two decades, the United Nations has constructed a firm foundation for carrying out its mandate to protect the rights of all members of the human family. It was a major force in the 1950s and in the 1960s in guiding many of the Afro-Asian colonies to independence. Hundreds of millions of Third World peoples who had been dominated by outside forces for so long obtained their human right of independence in these two decades. The UN played a major role in this historic accomplishment.

The magnificent accomplishments of the 1950s and the 1960s were noted in the very being of the UN. The late Secretary General U Thant said, "The promotion and protection of human rights form the very essence and provide the deepest meaning and motivation of the UN as an international organization."

The Charter of the UN refers to human rights in its preamble and in six different articles. The preamble eloquently states that the peoples of the UN express their determination "to reaffirm forth in fundamental human rights in the dignity and worth of the human person in equal rights of men and women and of nations large and small."

The Charter, adopted at the San Francisco Conference in 1945, was reinforced in the mandate to be concerned about the rights of all the members of the family of man by the Universal Declaration of Human Rights. On December 10, 1948, the General Assembly thoroughly committed the UN to "a common standard of achievement for all peoples and all nations" in the area of human rights.

In the past few years, the cause of human rights has suffered because the UN has practiced selective outrage. South African apartheid is clearly a gross violation of human rights. No one concerned about human values could say otherwise, and the UN has spoken and taken various actions on this matter.

But on Uganda, where the international news media have accurately reported the human suffering of the people under Amin, the United Nations has not taken any action. Why the selective outrage? Why the double standard?

For the sake of maintaining some semblance of credibility, the

178

United Nations must seize the initiative. But more importantly, for the sake of the Ugandan people who have suffered too long under the rule of a murderer. The United Nations has the universal mandate and the power; it must assume leadership to bring the nightmare to an end.

With the inauguration of President Carter in 1977, an increased impetus was given to human rights. While there is a difference of opinion as to certain democratic rights like freedom of the press, opposition political parties, and an independent judicial system, no responsible group denies that torture, murder and genocide are violations of human rights. Amin's reign constitutes a gross violation of the human rights of the Ugandan people. His propensity to liquidate people is similar to Hitler's.

The United Nations has the precious universal mandate to fight against gross and extreme violations of human rights. The organization must act as a standard for human rights, retaining its world force only if it is applied equally and universally. Otherwise the UN becomes the tool of hypocrisy.

We call upon the United States and other countries as members of the United Nations to exercise every action to bring this about in the UN. The silence by the UN on the Uganda issue is so painful that member countries must inform the organization that unless immediate action is taken, they will postpone their payments to the organization. It would be a grievous disservice to human rights for members not to express their dissatisfaction with some form of serious action.

The agonies of the hundreds of thousands of Ugandans brutalized by Amin call out for a response. The United Nations as the representative of the world community is compelled to take immediate action to end this agony.

Individual countries and leaders have spoken. The Commonwealth of States declared itself in June 1977. The Organization of African Unity at its July 1977 meeting in Gabon was disappointingly silent on Amin. Now the one universal organization has the opportunity to aggressively pursue actions to end the horrors going on in Uganda under Amin. The United Nations must act or suffer the very serious consequences to its credibility.

History recorded six and a half ugly years between the time

that Hitler took power in early 1933 and that fateful day in September 1939 when he pushed Europe into a bloodbath that would eventually extend to the world.

Amin took over in early 1971. History has already given him six and a half years. What will the world community do?

Hitler, within a few weeks of becoming the dictator of Nazi Germany, launched on April 1, 1933, the first official public campaign against the Jews. On that day, the Nazis had organized their first anti-Jewish boycott.

Amin waited more than several months before he struck out with brutality against the Jews. He did it in the spring of 1972.

Hitler later persecuted other minority groups and the Christian churches. Amin, who has proclaimed his admiration for Hitler, has followed the same path.

On June 23, 1977, after it was known that in the previous week hundreds of Ugandans had disappeared and more had fled into neighboring Kenya, Radio Uganda said, "President Amin has been resting after a long period of hard work." Another broadcast said that he was enjoying a second honeymoon.

Between 1933 and 1939, while the Nazis killed, they also celebrated. Goering's wedding in 1935 in Berlin was hailed as one of the great social events of that decade in Europe.

The international community must assume its moral responsibility to end the suffering and agony of the Ugandan peoples. The new Hitler—Idi Amin—can only bring about a conflict that will bring death and suffering to all of Africa.

The long months since our departure from Uganda in early 1973 have at least seen one change—there is little doubt that Amin is a brutal tyrant.

In the months from April to September 1973, while still the U.S. ambassador to Uganda, and completing my consultations in Washington, D.C., I maintained the position that the U.S. should, once the official Americans were withdrawn and the private American community significantly reduced, close its embassy in Kampala. This action, I believed, would be a sign of our official disgust with the ongoing genocide taking place.

Within a short time after our return to academic life in the fall of 1973, the U.S. government did close the embassy in Kampala.

There was, however, a reluctance by the Department of State to give the ongoing genocide as the official primary reason. References were made to internal security problems for U.S. personnel at the embassy. Previously, the department referred to Amin's unacceptable statements on Vietnam.

But at least the U.S. Embassy in Kampala was closed. Once back in academic life and convinced that Amin was a brutal tyrant, I began writing and lecturing on the subject. The three years from 1973–1976 were lean from the standpoint of American interest in Amin, the brutal tyrant. While several specialized journals and magazines like *America, Worldview*, and the *Christian Science Monitor* published my articles on Amin, several were turned down.

In November 1975, a national journal told me that my article on Amin was "too emotional." In addition to calling on all countries to withdraw their embassies from Kampala, I had written:

> What can people do? In a world where high ranking diplomats give a standing ovation to a murderer, it is easy for ordinary citizens to despair of what can be done. As citizens we can speak out against Amin. We can write letters, lecture, initiate boycotts and otherwise manifest our strong disapproval of him.
>
> An example of a people's reaction occurred that same first week of October when Amin was at the UN. The Spanish government executed five terrorists convicted of murdering policemen. Within hours, demonstrations of protest flared up across Europe. In that week every European government but Iceland had recalled its ambassador from Madrid or kept him home for consultations.
>
> One cannot help raise the question as to why the Spanish execution of five terrorists could arouse such reaction and at the same time a murderer of thousands could visit Europe, call on the UN, advocate the extinction of a state, and witness no visible opposition.
>
> If ordinary people had been aware of Amin's record, there could have been a series of actions. These could have included the refusal of airport personnel to be involved in his arrival, the refusal of waiters to serve his reception. In these simple non-violent ways, the disgust of people would have been manifested.

In the final analysis, the first step for nations, diplomats, ordinary people, is to recognize the evil that is before us. Let it not be said that we did not have the courage to recognize a human tragedy and to characterize it as it was. Finally, I submit to my fellow believers of all faiths that we pray for the Ugandan peoples in their hour of oppression.

While the above was rejected in 1975 along with other similar articles, a change began in 1977. There emerged a clear acceptance of the fact of Amin's brutality. This was at least an improvement over the days of Hitler, when in 1939, six years after he took over, many in the world still spoke of him as a folk hero!

We credit much of this awareness of what Amin is to the international media, not to governments. Thanks to almost instant and thorough reporting by the media, the world community has been kept appraised of Amin's butchering of his own people. The world press has carried out its mission of reporting the news.

Now the people of the world community must insist that their governments act. We call upon all governments to follow the examples of the United States and Great Britain and immediately withdraw their diplomatic missions from Uganda. Amin's henchmen who are serving as his representatives overseas should also be expelled.

The one organization that has the sanction of the international community to act is the United Nations. We call on each member of the United Nations to insist that the world organization end the brutal regime of Amin. Major powers like the United States have a special obligation to use their influence with the UN and its specialized agencies to act.

Idi Amin is the new Hitler in Africa.

Idi Amin, a pistol strapped to his hip, attending the July 4, 1977, meeting of the Organization of African Unity in Libreville, Gabon.

BOOKS BY THOMAS PATRICK MELADY

Profiles of African Leaders
White Man's Future In Black Africa
Faces of Africa
Kenneth Kaunda of Zambia
Revolution of Color
Western Policy and The Third World
Development: Lessons for the Future **(coauthor)**
Burundi: The Tragic Years

BOOKS BY MARGARET BADUM MELADY

Leopold Sedar Senghor: Rhythm and Reconciliation

BOOKS BY THOMAS AND MARGARET MELADY

House Divided
Uganda: The Asian Exiles

184